Collins



Enhanced

# Science Now

A Science Textbook based on Holistic Learning Theory

# 5

Name : ..........................................................................................

Grade : .............................. Section : ........................................................

Even though I've been reclassified as a dwarf planet, I still have something fascinating to reveal. On my surface lies a heart-shaped feature called "Tombaugh Regio," a vast icy plain named after my discoverer, Clyde Tombaugh.

What am I? ..............................................

**Series Editor | Jyothsna Natraj**

HarperCollins*Publishers*

*Publishing operations in 17 countries and 120+ imprints globally*

William Collins' dream of knowledge for all began with the publication of his first book in 1819. A self-educated mill worker, he not only enriched millions of lives, but also founded a flourishing publishing house. Today, staying true to this spirit, Collins books are packed with inspiration, innovation and practical expertise. They place you at the centre of a world of possibility and give you exactly what you need to explore it.

Published by Collins Learning
An imprint of HarperCollins*Publishers* India
Building No. 10, Tower A, 4th Floor, DLF Cyber City, Gurugram, Haryana 122002, India

First edition 2024
Reprint edition: 2025
ISBN: 978-93-6213-596-4

Content developed by **Excelsoft Technologies Pvt Ltd.**
Artwork, typesetting and layout by **AptaraCorp Ltd., Mammoth Studioz Ltd, iBook Services**
Printed and bound in India by Saurabh Printers Pvt. Ltd.

**ACKNOWLEDGEMENTS**

**Title Page:** Elen11

**Inside:** Page **4:** Tomas Knopp; **10:** Przemek Klos, Ethan Daniels, chinahbzyg, Oksana Alekseeva; **13:** ChaiyonS021, David Lade; **19:** Jerry Horbert, Oksana Alekseeva, MVPhoto, chinahbzyg; **20:** Jena Ardell; **33:** Wild Horse Photography, Ian Gethings; **46:** Muhammad Owais Khan; **58:** Joao Paulo Burini; **67:** Jose Luis Pelaez Inc, Images By Tang Ming Tung, MoMo Productions; **69:** Godruma; **81:** Jonathan Knowles; **82:** Excelsoft; **86:** eddtoro ; **93:** Maciej Frolow; **103:** Tetiana Lazunova, iNueng, KanKhem; **105:** fotostory, Cico; **107:** Igor Zh.; **108:** stockphoto mania; **109:** vallefrias; **114:** Sellwell; **115:** Simon Krzic, Mr Doomits; **116:** Catmando, Jiang Zhongyan, Siim Sepp, Siim Sepp; **117:** sonsam, J.Schelkle, Siim Sepp, Siim Sepp; **118:** nito, Siim Sepp, Alaettin YILDIRIM, Tyler Boyes; **119:** teena137, hxdbzxy, idea for life, anat chant, Imfoto; **124:** Excelsoft, Excelsoft; **125:** F.J. Jimenez, cako74, Artis777; **135:** Kin Lush, Floortje; **137:** Andrey_Kuzmin, konzeptm; **143:** Andrey_Kuzmin, konzeptm; **144:** mgkaya, rolfo allgaeu; **158:** Yuji Sakai, posteriori; **167:** ajt, OlFedv; **168:** MB Photography, Life On White, MarcelC, Paul Starosta, Pornpimon Lekudom, TexBr

**Supplementary Booklet:** dumayne, Richard Drury, Icon_Craft_Studio, Olesia Kononenko, Julia_Sudnitskaya, IconicBestiary, ilviaggiatore, Tahreer Photography, Fiordaliso; AlionaManakova, pijama61, sarunyu_foto, eliflamra, AlionaManakova, sarunyu_foto



Browse the complete Collins catalogue at www.collins.in.
For any queries/feedback, please write to us at SCHOOLSUPPORT@harpercollins.co.in.

# Preface

We live in a rapidly changing world where a person's decision can have an impact on the environment and others. Should the learning approach remain the same? What type of learning and skills should be developed so that students can face the demands and challenges of everyday life and succeed in the 21st century? One way of achieving this would be adopting the *holistic learning theory*.

*Holistic learning theory* or *holistic education* implies that each person finds identity, meaning and purpose in life through connections to the community, to the natural world and to values such as compassion and peace. It strives to help learners grow in all dimensions: intellectual, emotional, social, artistic, moral, psychological, physical, aesthetic, creative, intuitive and spiritual.

***Enhanced Science Now***, a series of eight books for Classes 1 to 8, adheres to the guidelines of the *National Education Policy* (NEP) 2020 and adopts the *holistic learning theory*. This enhanced edition retains the focus of the original edition, where the development of lateral thinking, analytical, research and deduction skills in students were encouraged. While the strong content would help strengthen the knowledge of the core science subject, new features based on the holistic learning theory would help in the development of every student's intellectual, emotional, social, artistic and creative potentials. This enhanced edition, thus, is an attempt to provide meaningful learning and help the students become well-rounded adults, ready to face the challenges in the 21st century, and ultimately empower the students to discover their full potential as learners.

## Key Features

- **Summary** Snapshot of the chapter in the form of a graphic organizer for quick revision
- **Exercise** Questions dealing with Remembering and Understanding levels of Bloom's taxonomy
- **Cognitive Corner** Section dealing with Applying, Analysing, Evaluating and Creating levels of Bloom's taxonomy and Life Skills
- **Worksheets** Pictorial exercises based on the United Nations Sustainable Development Goals
- **Skills You Need** A variety of interesting information and activities to introduce skill courses with some form of experiential learning
- **Happiness Activity Sheets** A variety of interesting activities based on life skills, self-awareness, other awareness, emotional needs and mental needs
- **Vernacular Names** List of plants and animals used in the book and their names in a few Indian regional languages
- **STEAM Activities** Engaging STEAM-based activities for the future problem solvers, critical thinkers, innovators and inventors

Four **assessment papers** and two **comprehensive assessment papers** have been given, in addition to the exercises at the end of each chapter.

The **Series Editor** for classes 1 to 5 is **Jyothsna Natraj**, a teacher at Vidya Mandir Senior Secondary School. She has been teaching science for over a decade. She has experience in web-based content development and has extensively used technologies such as 'SMART' tools in her classes.

Feedback, valuable comments and suggestions from the users are welcome.

**Authors**

# Key Features

The key features of ***Enhanced Science Now*** are completely aligned with the **National Education Policy** (NEP) 2020, and have been designed based on the *holistic learning theory* to facilitate a holistic education. These features not only aim at the development of intellectual capabilities of the students but also aim at the development of physical capabilities, intellectual abilities, cognitive or mental abilities, emotional abilities and social skills.

Multifaceted features such as Cognitive Corner, Life Skills, Worksheet, Skills You Need, Happiness Activity Sheets and STEAM Activities would help in the holistic development of a student through interesting questions, projects and activities while providing experiential learning and fostering innovative thinking and creativity.

The series also aims at making the students aware of the **Sustainable Developments Goals (SDGs)**. The SDGs are the 17 Global Goals adopted by all United Nations Member States in 2015 to help end poverty, protect the planet and ensure peace and prosperity for all by 2030. Read more about the goals at https://www.un.org/sustainabledevelopment/

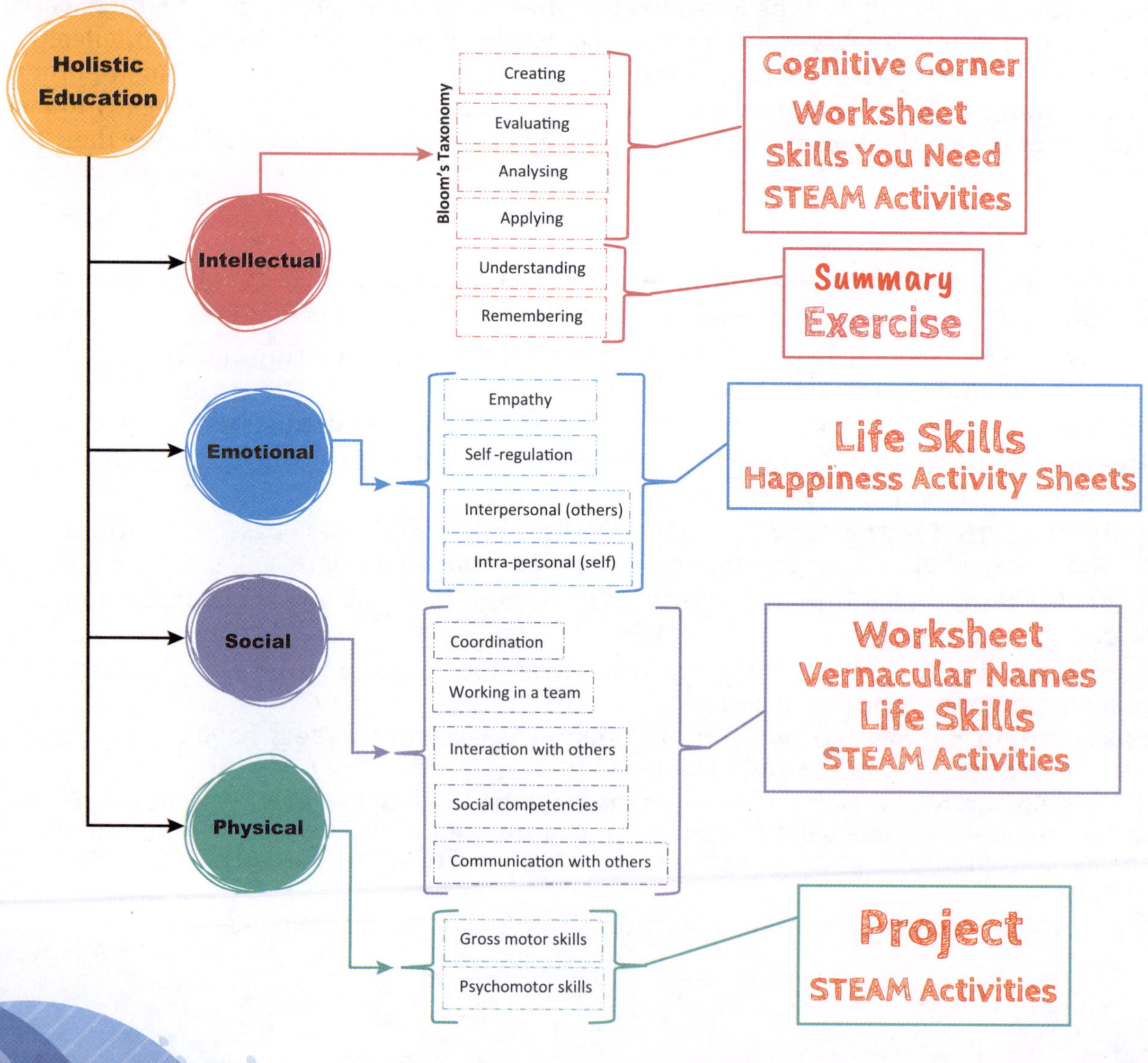

# About the Features

## Summary

Snapshot of the chapter in the form of a graphic organizer for quick revision

## Exercise

Questions dealing with Remembering and Understanding levels of Bloom's taxonomy

## Cognitive Corner

Section dealing with Applying, Analysing, Evaluating and Creating levels of Bloom's taxonomy

| | |
|---|---|
| **Critical Thinking** | Questions to address cognitive development such as thinking, reasoning, analysis, inference and drawing conclusions |
| **Picture Study** | Questions to help develop observation and inference skills |
| **Project** | Ideas for experiential learning and subject enrichment with cross-curricular links |

## Life Skills

Thought-provoking passage and relevant questions to help develop sensible life skills such as self-awareness, empathy and attitude towards self and others

## Worksheet

Pictorial exercises at the end of each chapter based on the United Nations Sustainable Development Goals

Collins | SUSTAINABLE DEVELOPMENT GOALS

Collins Learning supports the Sustainable Development Goals

## Skills You Need

A variety of interesting information and activities to introduce skill courses with some form of experiential learning

## Happiness Activity Sheets

A variety of interesting activities based on life skills, self-awareness, other awareness, emotional needs and mental needs

## Vernacular Names

List of plants and animals used in the book and their names in a few Indian regional languages

## STEAM Activities

Engaging STEAM-based activities for the future problem solvers, critical thinkers, innovators and inventors

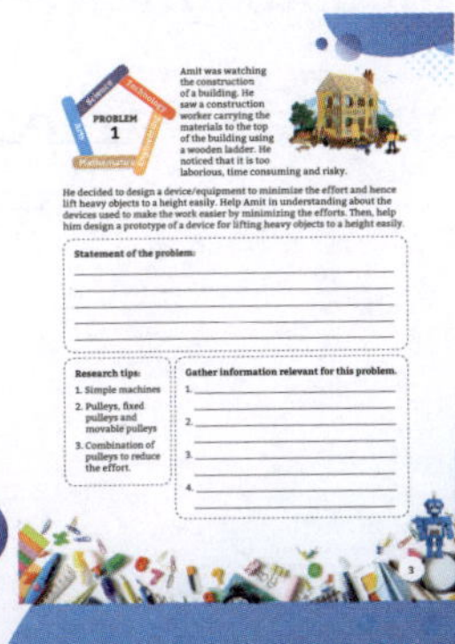
PROBLEM 1

Amit was watching the construction of a building. He saw a construction worker carrying the materials to the top of the building using a wooden ladder. He noticed that it is too laborious, time consuming and risky.

He decided to design a device/equipment to minimize the effort and hence lift heavy objects to a height easily. Help Amit in understanding about the devices used to make the work easier by minimizing the efforts. Then, help him design a prototype of a device for lifting heavy objects to a height easily.

Statement of the problem:

Research tips:
1. Simple machines
2. Pulleys, fixed pulleys and movable pulleys
3. Combination of pulleys to reduce the effort.

Gather information relevant for this problem.
1.
2.
3.
4.

3

# Contents

# 1 Growing Plants

## Learning Checklist

- New plants from seeds, roots, stems, leaves and spores
- Agriculture

## Let's Get Started

Look at the pictures of the fruits given below. Write whether each of these fruits have no seed, one seed, few seeds or many seeds.

______________________

______________________

______________________

______________________

______________________

______________________

New plants mostly grow from seeds. Seeds are formed from flowers. So, we can say that seeds help the plant to reproduce. However, there are some plants that do not produce seeds. How do they reproduce then?

In this chapter, let us learn about the various ways in which plants reproduce.

# NEW PLANTS FROM SEEDS

Most fruits and vegetables have seeds. New plants grow from these seeds. Let us do an activity to understand the structure of a seed.

**Science in Context**

A flower has pollen grains that help in the formation of seeds.

## Activity 1

**Aim:** To remove the seed coat and observe the structures inside a seed

**Materials required:** Some kidney beans (*rajma*), water and a plate

**Procedure:**

1. Soak some kidney beans overnight in water.
2. The next day, you will see that the seeds have absorbed water and look swollen.
3. Remove the outer covering of the seeds.

This outer covering is called the seed coat. Now, let us study the structure inside the seed.

The seed coat protects the seed and the baby plant inside it. There is a tiny opening in the seed coat, called the **micropyle**, through which the seed absorbs water. Above the **micropyle** is a scar called **hilum**, which shows the place where seed was attached to the fruit. The structure inside the seed coat can be separated into two halves. Each half is called a **cotyledon** or **seed leaf**. The seed leaves store food for the developing baby plant, also called an **embryo**. Seeds such as peas, pulses and beans have two cotyledons. Seeds such as maize, rice and wheat have only one cotyledon. In these seeds, food is stored in a special tissue called **endosperm**.

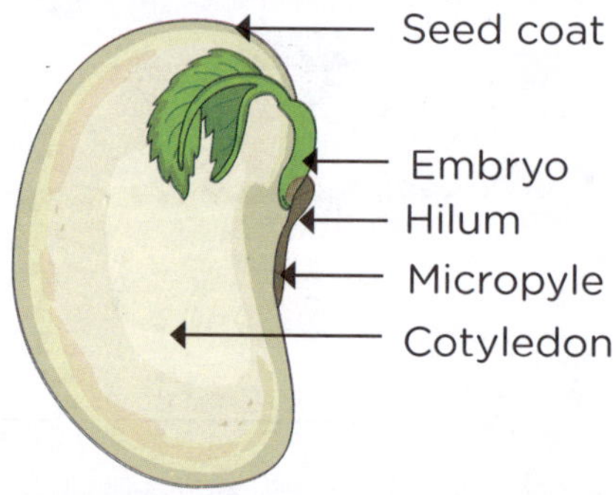

Parts of a seed

**Science in Context**

Seeds with two cotyledons are called dicot seeds while seeds with only one cotyledon are called monocot seeds.

Not all seeds grow into new plants. Some seeds are destroyed by harsh weather conditions, such as strong winds and heavy rain, while some are eaten by birds and animals as food. A seed needs sufficient amount of water, light, warmth and air to grow into a new plant. The process in which a new plant grows from a seed is called **germination**.

The stages of germination in a seed are given below.

- A seed sown in soil gets warmth, air, light and water.
- The seed coat breaks and a baby plant emerges. The baby plant grows small roots which develop further.
- A small shoot develops in the plant.
- As the roots and the shoot grow in size, leaves appear, and the cotyledons shrink and eventually fall off.

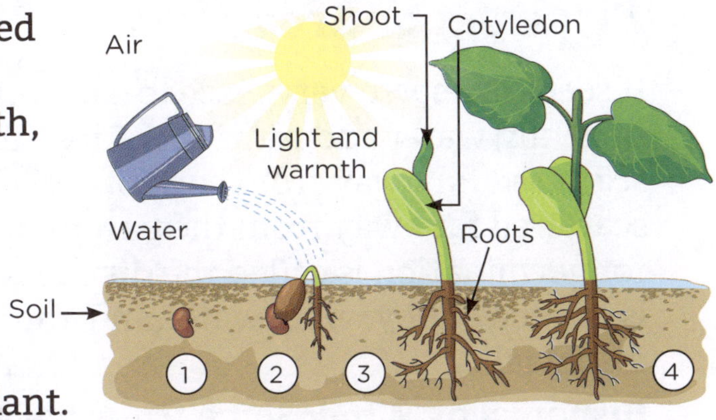

Stages of germination in a seed

## Activity 2

**Aim:** To study the conditions necessary for the germination of seeds

**Materials required:** Bean seeds, a bowl, three plastic containers, cotton cloth, foil paper and water

**Procedure:**

**Set-up 1:**

- Soak a few bean seeds in a bowl of water for about 30 minutes.
- Dampen a cotton cloth with water and place it in a plastic container.
- Place the soaked seeds in a plastic container and cover it with foil paper.
- Then, place the container in a dark place and leave it undisturbed for two days.

**Set-up 2:**

- Take a handful of seeds in a plastic container and add enough water to it so that the seeds float in the water.
- Place the plastic container under sunlight, undisturbed, for two days.

**Set-up 3:**

- Take a handful of seeds in a plastic container and close it with a lid.
- Keep the plastic container near a window. Leave it undisturbed for two days.

**Observation:** Fill in the table based on your observations.

| Experimental set-up | Conditions | Observation |
|---|---|---|
| Set-up 1 | | |
| Set-up 2 | | |
| Set-up 3 | | |

**Conclusion:** ____________________ and ____________________ are necessary for the germination of seeds.

## Dispersal of Seeds

If seeds are sown very close to each other, they will struggle for space, light, air, water and nutrients. Therefore, it is necessary that the seeds are scattered far away from each other. The process in which the seeds are scattered far away from the parent plant to obtain suitable conditions for germination is called the **dispersal of seeds**. In nature, seed dispersal is carried out by wind, water and animals. They are called agents of seed dispersal.

**Dispersal by Wind:** Some fruits have very light and hairy or wing-shaped seeds that get caught in the wind and are easily blown away to far-off places. These seeds germinate in fertile soil if they get favourable conditions. Some of the plants whose seeds are dispersed by wind are dandelion, cotton and maple.

Dandelion

Coconut

**Dispersal by Water:** Seeds of some fruits have a waterproof covering, and they are so light that they can float on water and can be carried to far-off places. For example, the coconut has a heavy seed inside, but it floats on water, as the seed is covered by spongy layers of fibre filled with air. The seed dispersal of lotus, water lily and mangrove takes places with the help of water.

**Dispersal by Animals:** Some seeds have hook-like structures that help them cling on to animals' fur or have sticky substances that stick to animals' skin. This way, the seeds are carried away from the parent plant. Many birds and animals eat fruits along with their seeds. The seeds come out of their bodies in their droppings and are scattered to different places where they grow into new plants. Examples of plants whose seeds are dispersed by animals are cocklebur, mistletoe and berries.

Cocklebur

**Dispersal by Explosion:** Some seeds have a leathery covering, or are found inside pods that explode or split open when exposed to the sun, or when they dry up, or even when they are touched. When the pods burst open, the seeds are scattered far away from the parent plant. Examples of plants whose seeds are dispersed by explosion include pea, gorse, peanut, balsam and castor.

Peas

## Revise and Recall

**Match the seeds with their corresponding dispersal method.**

| | |
|---|---|
| 1. Cotton | (a) Water |
| 2. Gorse | (b) Wind |
| 3. Coconut | (c) Animal |
| 4. Berries | (d) Explosion |

New plants can grow not only from seeds, but also from roots, stems, leaves and spores. This is called vegetative propagation. Let us learn how.

# NEW PLANTS FROM ROOTS

Roots of plants, such as sweet potato, carrot and beetroot, store food. These roots contain small buds[1] from which new plants grow. A piece of the root, along with the bud, is cut and planted in the soil. Under suitable conditions, these buds develop roots and shoot, forming a whole new plant.

# NEW PLANTS FROM STEMS

a

Various natural and artificial methods can be used to obtain new plants from stems. Some of them are discussed below.

Carrot

### Word Web

[1]**Bud:** a small lump on the plant part from which new shoot, leaf, flower or a new plant can grow

**Underground Stems:** Some plants have stems that grow below the ground. Such stems are called underground stems. For example, potato, ginger and onion. These stems have small buds on them. In potatoes, these buds are known as the **eyes**. Any portion of a potato with an eye can grow into a new plant.

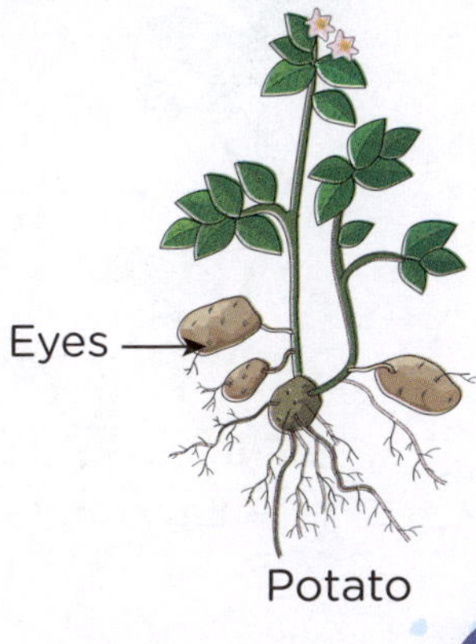


Potato

**Stem Cutting:** In plants such as rose, *Bougainvillea* and money plant, a part of the stem containing a bud is cut and planted in the soil. It develops roots after some time and finally grows into a whole new plant. This method is called **stem cutting**.

Stem cutting

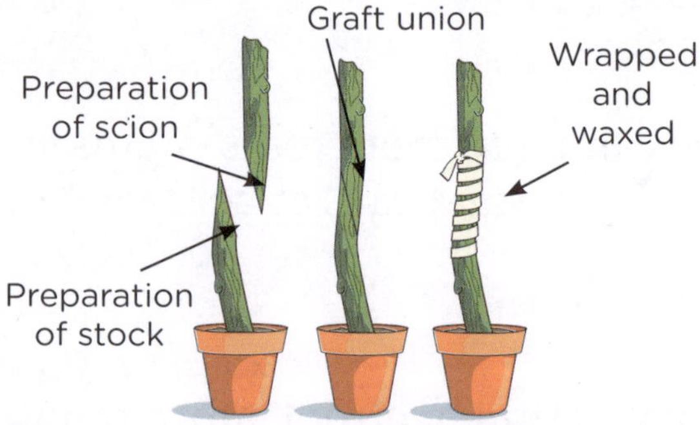

Grafting

**Grafting:** In plants such as rose, mango and apple, a portion of the shoot is cut and then attached to the shoot of another plant. The part of the stem that is cut is called the **scion** and the part to which it is attached is called the **stock**. This method is called **grafting**.

**Layering:** In plants such as jasmine and raspberry, a branch of the plant is bent until it touches the ground. A portion of it is covered with soil, leaving the growing tip exposed. The portion covered with soil develops roots after a few days. It is then cut from the parent plant and it then grows as an independent plant. This method is called **layering**.

Plants such as strawberry also reproduce through layering as they have horizontal stems that grow near the ground. These stems are called **runners**. They form roots at regular intervals and produce new plants.

Layering

Runners

## NEW PLANTS FROM LEAVES AND SPORES

In plants such as *Bryophyllum* and *Begonia*, new plantlets can grow from the well-developed leaves while these leaves are still attached to the branch of the plant. Once these plantlets develop, they drop off or detach themselves from the parent plant. They then grow into new plants on moist soil.

*Bryophyllum*

In some plants, such as ferns and mosses, new plants grow from special structures called **spores**[1]. These are very light and tiny, powdery structures. They can survive for a long period of time in unfavourable conditions.

Ferns

**Word Web**

[1]**Spores:** tiny seeds that appear powdery when touched

## AGRICULTURE

A plant grown in large numbers on a plot of land during a particular season is called a **crop**.

The practice of growing crops on a large scale in fields is called **agriculture**.

**Science in Context**

Around one-third of the human population is involved in agriculture.

There are various steps involved in agriculture.

1. **Preparing the soil by ploughing the field:** Farmers use **bullocks** or **tractors** to plough their fields. Ploughing turns the soil and loosens it.

Ploughing using bullocks

Ploughing using tractor

2. **Adding manure or fertilizers to the soil:** When farmers grow crops year after year, the soil becomes less fertile. So, farmers add natural manure or chemical fertilizers to increase the fertility of the soil.

**Science in Context**

To increase the fertility of the soil, farmers often plant different variety of crops in a field in successive years. The nutrients used by one type of crop is restored by planting the other variety. This method is called crop rotation. For example, legumes are alternated with cereals to maintain soil fertility.

3. **Sowing healthy, good-quality seeds:** Healthy seeds are sown either manually in the grooves made by the farmers while preparing the field, or through machines called seed drills.

Manual sowing

Seed drill

4. **Irrigation (watering) of land:** Watering the land regularly for the crops to grow well is called **irrigation**. Modern methods of irrigation, such as sprinklers, are common nowadays.

Sprinkler

5. **Protecting the land from weeds[1] and pests[2]:** The farmland is protected from weeds and pests by spraying chemicals called weedicides and pesticides, respectively.

Spraying chemicals

**Word Web**

[1]**Weeds:** unwanted plants growing among crops

[2]**Pests:** insects and animals that harm the crops

6. **Harvesting:** The fully grown crops are cut and collected for use. This process is called harvesting. Harvesting can be done manually, or with the help of machines called **harvesters**.
7. **Storing:** Harvested crops are stored in dry, well-ventilated places that are free from germs and pests.

Manual harvesting

Using a harvester

Storage

Different crops need different climatic conditions to grow. Some crops grow well in hot climate while some grow well in cold climate; some need less water to grow while some need a lot of water, and hence, grow well in areas that receive heavy rainfalls. Therefore, farmers grow crops based on the climate suitable for each of them.

**Go Green**

Growing plants in barren lands not only adds to the production of food to meet human needs, but also gives us pure air and prevents soil erosion.

Depending on the time of the year or the season in which they are grown, crops are of two main types: kharif and rabi.

**Kharif crops:** Kharif crops are usually sown in the beginning of June and harvested in September–October. These crops are grown during this season because they need plenty of water for good yield, which they get from the monsoon rains.

Examples of kharif crops are cotton, maize, paddy, sunflower, soybean and millet.

**Rabi crops:** Rabi crops are grown in winter from November and harvested in April. These crops do not require much water for growth.

Examples of rabi crops are cauliflower, beans, peas, wheat, mustard, gram, barley and oats.

## Keywords

**Seed coat:** The outer covering of a seed that protects the structure inside it

**Cotyledon:** The part of the seed that contains food for the baby plant

**Embryo:** The part of the seed from which a new plant grows under suitable conditions

**Micropyle:** A tiny opening in the seed coat

**Dispersal:** The process in which seeds are scattered far away from the parent plant that helps in getting suitable conditions for germination

**Agriculture:** The practice of growing crops on a large scale in fields

**Harvesting:** The process of cutting and collecting fully grown crops from fields for use

**Kharif crops:** Crops that are grown during the monsoon season, that is, from June to October

**Rabi crops:** Crops that are grown during the winter season, that is, from November to April

## Summary

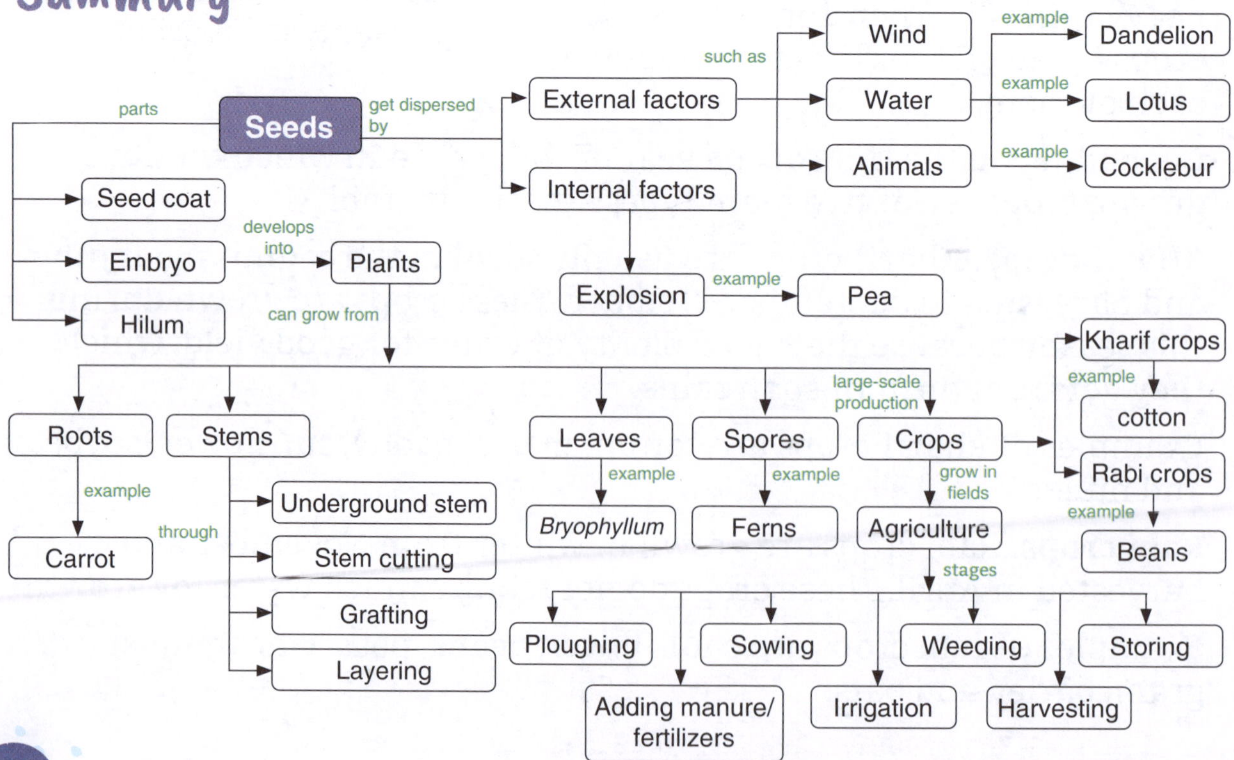

# Exercise

W

## A. Choose the correct option for each of the following.

ia

1. The part of a seed from which a new plant grows is ________.
   (a) hilum (b) cotyledon (c) embryo (d) seed coat
2. The seeds of ________ plants are dispersed by wind.
   (a) cocklebur (b) berries (c) mistletoe (d) cotton
3. ________ plant can reproduce through stem cutting.
   (a) *Bougainvillea* (b) *Bryophyllum*
   (c) Carrot (d) Bean
4. Kharif crops are usually grown during the months of ________.
   (a) June–August (b) June–October
   (c) November–April (d) November–January
5. Pea and wheat are ________ crops.
   (a) rabi (b) kharif (c) both (d) None of these

## B. Fill in the blanks using the correct words.

ia

1. ________ seeds have one cotyledon. (Pea/Maize)
2. Seeds of ________ are dispersed away from the parent plant when their pods burst. (maple/peas)
3. ________ contain small buds called eyes from which new plants can grow. (Roses/Potatoes)
4. Tiny powdery structures seen on the leaves of ferns are called ________. (hooks/spores)
5. A ________ plant can be grown by layering. (rose/raspberry)

## C. Match the following.

| Column A | Column B |
|---|---|
| 1. Moss | (a) Dispersal by water |
| 2. Ginger | (b) New plant from roots |
| 3. Foxglove | (c) New plant from spores |
| 4. Cocklebur | (d) Underground stem |
| 5. Beetroot | (e) Dispersal by animals |

**D. State whether the following statements are true (T) or false (F).**

1. Dispersal of seeds avoids overcrowding of plants in one place.
2. Rose plant has plantlets on its leaves that grow into new plants.
3. In onion, new plants can be grown from the stem.
4. Irrigation is done before sowing the seeds into the soil.
5. Rabi crops depend on the monsoon rains for good yield.

**E. Answer the following in one word.**

1. The process in which a new plant grows from a seed
2. A dispersal agent for wing-shaped seeds
3. The process where a part of the stem containing a bud is cut and planted in the soil
4. Plants grown in large numbers on a plot of land during a particular season
5. The practice of growing crops on a large scale in fields

**F. Give reasons for the following.**

1. Seed leaves are important for a baby plant or embryo.
2. All seeds do not grow into new plants.
3. Scattering of seeds is important for the germination of a plant.
4 Strawberry plants also reproduce through layering.
5. Farmers alternately grow different varieties of crops.

**G. Answer the following questions briefly.**

1. What is the function of the seed coat?
2. What is germination?
3. What are the basic requirements for a seed to germinate?
4. What makes a coconut float on water although the seed inside it is heavy?
5. When does a fruit explode to disperse the seeds inside?
6. List three parts of plants other than seeds from which new plants can grow.
7. Name the two ploughing methods used by farmers.

**H. Answer the following questions.**

1. What is seed dispersal? Discuss the various agents of seed dispersal with suitable examples.

2. With the help of a diagram, explain the process of stem cutting and grafting.
3. How are crops grouped? Give two examples for each type.
4. List the various steps involved in agriculture. Explain the processes of irrigation and harvesting.

# Cognitive Corner

## Critical Thinking

1. Riya had kept her potted plant in a dark corner of her room. Her mother asked her to keep it near a window or in the balcony. Do you agree with her mother? If so, why?
2. Why do farmers add manure to the soil?

## Picture Study

Identify the plants in the following images and write down the method of seed dispersal that takes place in each of them.

1. 
2. 
3. 
4. 

## Project

Soak 3 or 4 beans overnight in a bowl. Plant them in a pot the next day. Observe after two or three days. Record your observations. Continue to observe the bean plants till they produce their own beans. Keep recording your observations periodically. Take photographs of each stage, then prepare a report and present it in your class.

## Life Skills

We can grow our own vegetables in a kitchen garden. Ask the elders in your family to make a small garden and grow a few vegetables. Kitchen wastes, such as vegetable peels, waste food, can be used to make manure for the plants. Water left after washing fruits, vegetables, rice and pulses can be used to water your plants.

List six of your favourite vegetables that you would like to grow in your kitchen garden.

12 RESPONSIBLE CONSUMPTION AND PRODUCTION

# Worksheet

To increase the crop production, farmers often use various chemicals such as pesticides and insecticides. These chemicals are very harmful to our health. With rain, these chemicals often get washed off and run-off to various water bodies resulting in pollution. Excessive use of chemicals also degrades the soil quality. Thus, the use of too much chemicals in agricultural practices leads to numerous problems.

To curb this, farmers are shifting to a new agricultural practice that involves lesser use of chemicals. This practice is called **organic farming**. In organic farming, biological fertilizers and pesticides obtained from plant and animal sources are used. Food and crops grown in this way are free of chemicals and do not harm our health. The biological fertilizers used in organic farming are environmentally safe and do not pollute soil and water.

An organic farm

Traditional agricultural practices not only lead to soil and water pollution through excessive use of chemicals, this sector is also responsible for the increased release of greenhouse gases.

A. What are greenhouse gases? Name any two greenhouse gases.

______________________________

______________________________

B. How does agriculture sector contribute to the increase in greenhouse gases?

______________________________

______________________________

C. Organic farming can reduce the release of greenhouse gases in agricultural practices. How?

______________________________

______________________________

# 2 Animal Habitats and Adaptations

## Learning Checklist

- Habitat
- Adaptation
- Migration

## Let's Get Started

The pictures given below show different animals in their natural environment. Choose from the given words and write the names of these places in the space provided.

| Forest | Pond | Desert | Polar region |
|---|---|---|---|

______________

______________

______________

______________

# HABITAT

The environment where an organism naturally lives and reproduces is called its **habitat**. Different organisms live in different habitats. They obtain food, shelter, air and water from their habitat.

Let us learn about the different types of habitats found on the Earth.

## Forest

Forest habitat

Forest habitats usually have a large number of plants and trees. A variety of animals live in forests in various places, such as caves (e.g., tiger and lion), on trees (e.g., birds and monkey), in burrows (e.g., snake and rabbit) and on the forest floor (e.g., deer, elephant and insects). Many animals that live in the forests have well-developed limbs[1] that help them to run and walk. Limbs also help them to hunt or run away from predators[2].

## Desert

Desert habitat

Desert habitats are sandy lands with scanty[3] rainfall. Most deserts are very hot and dry during the day and they become cold at night. Animals usually found in deserts are camel, kangaroo rat, rattlesnake, etc. Animals in deserts have special features to survive in that climate. For example, camels have thick, broad feet that help them walk easily on loose sand. They also have thick eyelids that protect their eyes from the sand blowing with the wind. They store water and fat in their humps for use in the times of scarcity. Some desert animals live in burrows to escape heat.

### Word Web

[1]**Limbs:** hands and legs

[2]**Predator:** an animal that kills and eats other animals

[3]**Scanty:** very little

### Science in Context

The Gobi desert in Asia and the deserts in the continent of Antarctica are always cold. They are called cold deserts.

## Polar Regions and Mountains

The high mountains and the Polar regions (the Arctic and Antarctic) are covered with snow and are very cold throughout the year. During winter, the temperature can drop to very low degrees. Some animals found in the Polar regions are polar bear, penguin, seal and walrus. Animals such as polar bears have thick fur on their body that keeps them warm. Penguins have a layer of fat under their skin, also called **blubber**. It helps in keeping their body warm.

Polar habitat

## Ocean

Oceans are the largest habitats of the world and contain salt water. Pacific Ocean, Arctic Ocean, Atlantic Ocean, Southern Ocean and Indian Ocean are the oceans on the Earth.

Big and small fish of different types are found in salt water habitats. Crabs, starfish, sharks, whales, prawns, sea turtles, sea horses, jellyfish, electric rays, octopuses and many other types of animals are found here.

Ocean habitat

## Freshwater

Freshwater habitats include various ponds, lakes, streams and rivers. Different kinds of fish, snakes and frogs live in this habitat. Frogs use their long hind legs and webbed feet for swimming in water. Water birds, such as ducks and swans, swim in the water with their webbed feet. Cranes have long legs to wade through water.

Pond: A freshwater habitat

# ADAPTATION

a

The features and habits of organisms that help them survive in their habitats are called **adaptation**. Let us learn about some adaptations of animals living in different habitats.

## Body Coverings

Animals have different types of body coverings, such as thick fur, scales and shell. Let us learn about them.

**Scales:** Bodies of reptiles, such as crocodile, lizard and snake are covered with scales. Snakes shed their skin periodically. The process of shedding of old skin to replace it with new skin is called **moulting**. The body of the fish is also covered with scales.

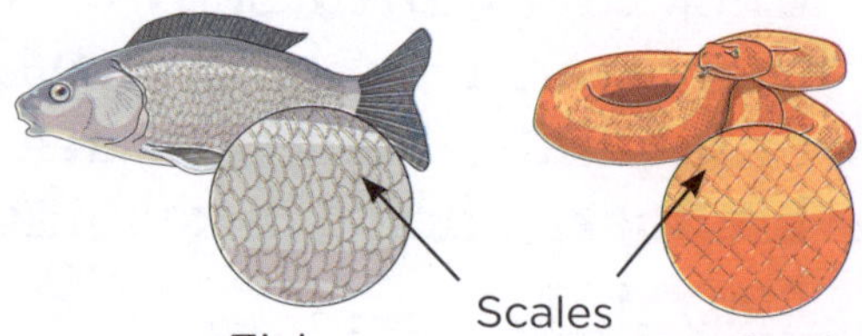


**Shell:** Shell protects the soft bodies of animals, such as turtle, tortoise and snail, from damage. The hard shell also protects them from being eaten by predators.

**Fur or Wool:** The body of animals such as polar bear and yak is covered with thick **fur**. A sheep's body is covered with **wool**. The fur/wool helps the animals to keep themselves warm in the cold weather.

**Feathers:** The body of birds is covered with feathers. Birds have three types of feathers:

**Flight feathers** are present on the wings and help birds fly.

**Body feathers** cover the body.

**Down feathers** keep the body warm.

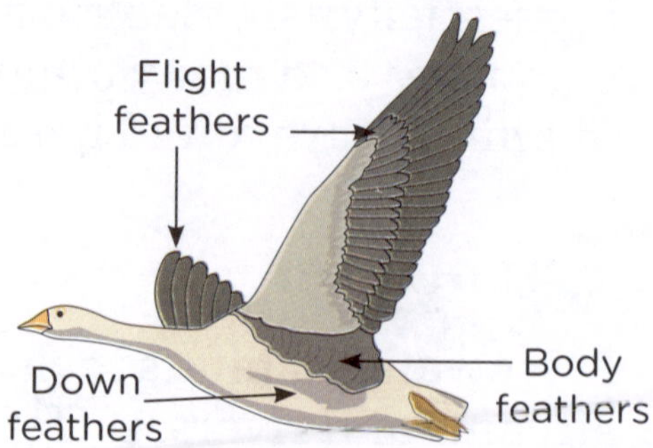


Bird

**Hard body covering:** Insects, such as the grasshopper and the cockroach, have a hard body covering made of a substance called **chitin**.

Cockroach

## Breathing Organs

Different animals have different breathing organs suited to their habitats.

**Skin:** Animals, such as earthworms, use their moist skin for breathing. The exchange of gases takes place through the surface of their skin. A frog breathes through its skin when it is inside water.

Earthworm breathes through skin

**Body surface:** Small microscopic[1] organisms breathe through their body surface. Examples are *Amoeba* and *Paramoecium*.

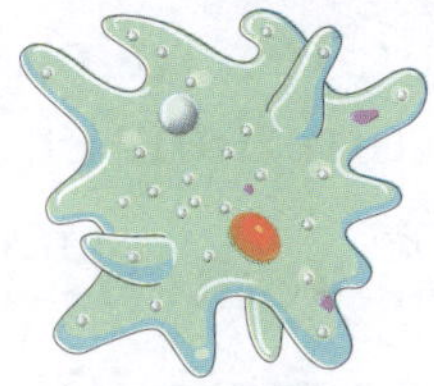

*Amoeba* breathes through body surface

### Word Web

[1]**Microscopic:** not large enough to be seen with the naked eye but visible under a microscope

**Gills:** Most aquatic animals, such as fish and prawns, breathe with the help of gills. Water flows in through the mouth and flows out through the gills. The gills help in absorbing the oxygen dissolved in water.

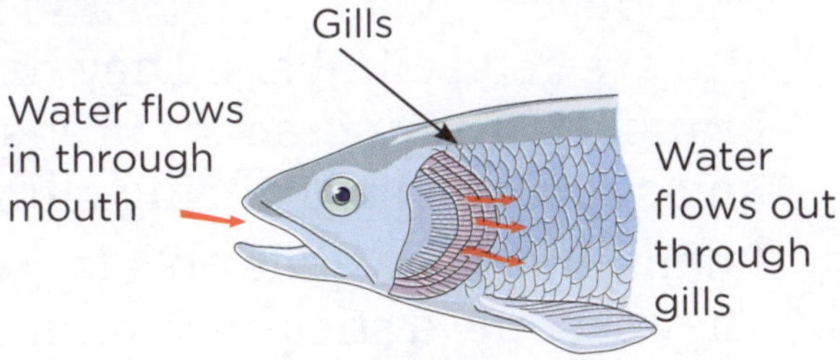


Fish breathe through gills

**Spiracles:** Insects have special structures for breathing known as **spiracles** (also called **air holes**). These are small openings present along the side of the insect's body. Air enters the insect's body through these spiracles and is expelled out through the same structures.

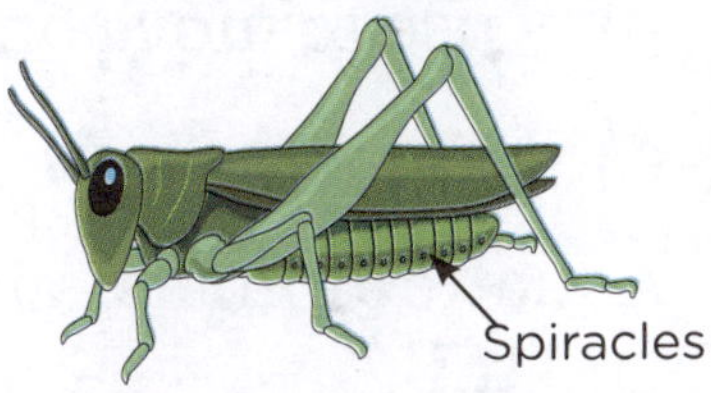


Insects breathe through spiracles

### Science in Context

The blood of insects is white in colour as it does not contain **haemoglobin** (the pigment that gives the red colour to our blood).

**Lungs:** Animals such as reptiles, birds and mammals take in air through their nose. The air that enters through the nose is carried to organs called **lungs**.

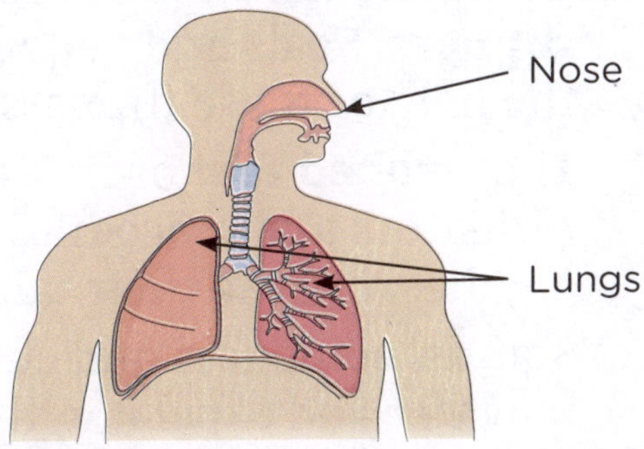


Breathing organs in humans

Amphibians such as frogs have a pair of lungs that help them to breathe on land and their moist skin helps them to breathe in water.

Frog

### Science in Context

Mammals such as dolphins and whales that live in the water also breathe through their lungs.

## Organs for Movement

a

Animals move around in search of food and shelter, to look for their mate and to escape from their enemies.

### Word Web

[1]**Secrete:** to produce and release

### Movement in Land Animals

The majority of animals that live on land move with the help of their legs (two at the front called **forelimbs**, and two at the back called **hindlimbs**). Kangaroos and frogs are good leapers. They have well-developed hindlimbs and short forelimbs. Monkeys live on trees and are good climbers. They have opposable thumb to hold onto branches. They possess a prehensile tail which coils around branches and supports them during climbing.

Snails and slugs glide on a large single foot. They secrete[1] a sticky substance that helps them in gliding. Centipedes have many legs which they use to move on land.

Snail

### Movement in Aquatic Animals

Aquatic animals, such as fish, move in water with the help of **fins** and **tail**.

Mammals such as dolphins, whales and porpoises have their forelimbs modified into **flippers**. Seals and penguins also swim with the help of these flippers.

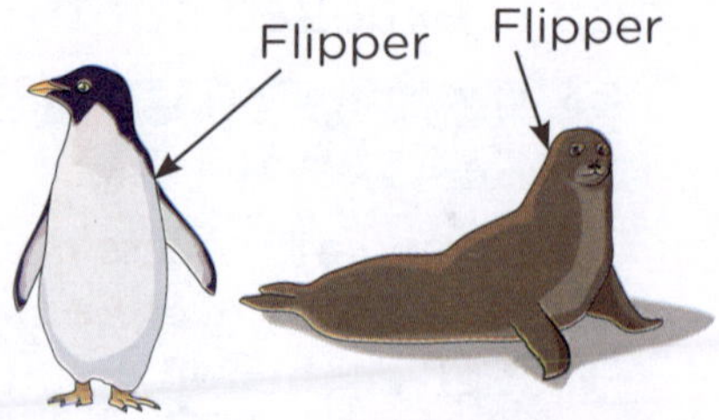


Penguin Seal

The **webbed feet** of frogs help them to swim. Alligators and crocodiles use their legs as paddles and use their tail for swimming.

Squids, octopuses and cuttlefish move by **jet propulsion**. They take in water and expel it with great force. When the water is expelled backwards, these animals move forward.

## Movement in Insects

Water boatman

Insects are small animals with six legs. Most insects have wings that help them to fly, while some do not have wings (e.g., spiders, bedbugs and ants) and move with the help of legs.

Insects, such as the grasshopper, hop with the help of their hind legs. Water boatman (a water insect) swims in water using its legs as oars[1].

## Movement in Birds

Birds fly with the help of their wings (forelimbs) covered with feathers.

These wings also have strong muscles that assist birds in their flight. These muscles are called **flight muscles**. The wings of a humming bird are very small and beat very fast. They help the bird hover in air while sucking nectar. Eagles have broad wings that help them glide in the air.

Movement in birds

**Science in Context**

Bat is the only mammal that can fly. Its wings are not made of feathers but of membranous skin stretched and connected to the forelimbs.

**Word Web**

[1]**Oar:** a long shaft of wood with a broad blade used for rowing boats

## Movement in Reptiles

Animals such as lizards and crocodiles crawl using their short legs.

Snakes do not have legs. They move with the help of scales and a flexible backbone, by pushing their body against the ground in a zig-zag manner.

Movement of a crocodile

Movement of a snake

## Movement in Humans

Human beings use their legs (hindlimbs) to stand, walk and run. Their hands (forelimbs) and the arrangement of their fingers help human beings hold objects and do various activities.

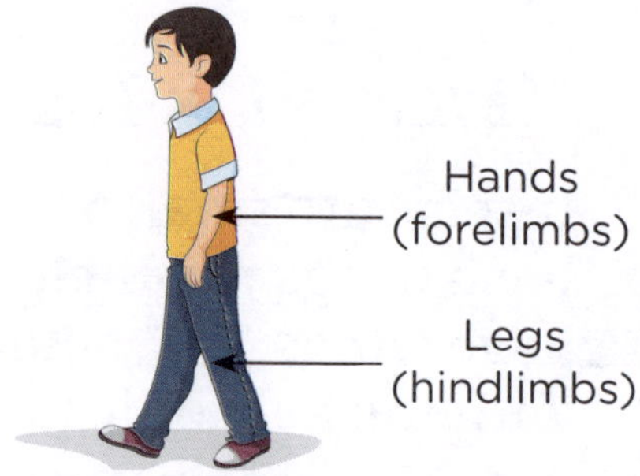


Movement of human beings

## Migration

The movement of animals in large groups from one place to another in search of food and warmth is called **migration**.

Some birds migrate during the winter season to reproduce and find food. They use the fat stored in their bodies on such long journeys.

Siberian white cranes or snow cranes migrate to India during the winters from Western Siberia.

Migration of Siberian cranes

Apart from birds, some mammals, such as whales, migrate during winter from the polar regions to the warmer oceans.

### Science in Context

The Arctic tern is a seabird that travels between the Arctic and Antarctic regions, which is almost 35,000 km in distance, in a year. It is also called the 'champion of migration'.

Some insects, such as monarch butterflies, migrate during winter from Canada to Mexico.

Salmon (a type of fish) migrate from seas to very long distances to lay their eggs in rivers. The European Eel migrates from river to sea to lay eggs.

### Revise and Recall

**State whether the following statements are true (T) or false (F).**

1. Prawns breathe with the help of gills.
2. Insects have only two spiracles for breathing.
3. Gills are the breathing organs of mammals.
4. Seals swim with the help of flippers.
5. A grasshopper hops with the help of its hind legs.

## Keywords

**Habitat:** The environment where an organism naturally lives and reproduces

**Adaptation:** The features and habits that help organisms to survive in their habitats

**Moulting:** The process of shedding old skin to replace it with new skin

**Spiracles:** The breathing organs of insects

**Blubber:** A thick layer of fat under the skin of animals that live in very cold places

**Migration:** The movement of animals in large groups from one place to another in search of food and warmth

## Summary

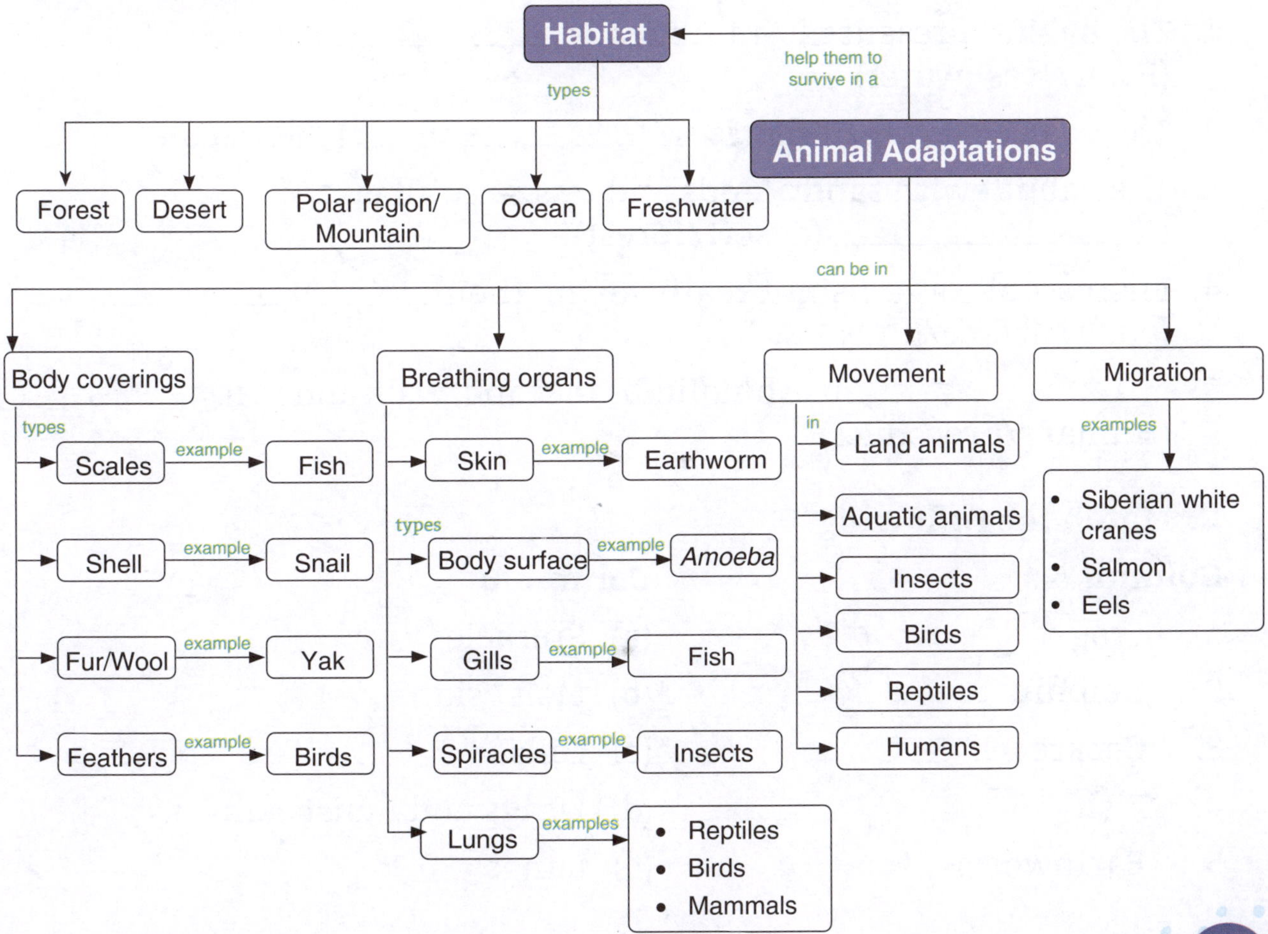

# Exercise

**A. Choose the correct option for each of the following.**

1. Identify the animal that belongs to the desert habitat.
   (a) Penguin (b) Seal (c) Camel (d) Walrus
2. Which of these is considered to be the largest habitat of the world?
   (a) Ocean (b) Forest (c) Desert (d) Freshwater
3. Jellyfish belong to which of these habitats?
   (a) Freshwater (b) Desert (c) Ocean (d) Polar
4. Identify the animal that has shell as its body covering.
   (a) Lizard (b) Tortoise (c) Yak (d) Crocodile
5. Which of these animals uses flippers for its movement?
   (a) Penguin (b) Lizard (c) Frog (d) Snake

**B. Fill in the blanks using the correct words.**

1. The habitat present in Antarctica is ________________. (Polar/freshwater)
2. The body covering of fish is ________________. (shell/scales)
3. The habitat with sandy lands and less rainfall is ________________. (desert/forest)
4. Microscopic organisms breathe using their ________________. (body surface/lungs)
5. ________________ use hindlimbs to stand, walk and run. (Humans/Crocodiles)

**C. Match the following.**

| Column A | Column B |
|---|---|
| 1. Frog | (a) Spiracles |
| 2. Dolphin | (b) Moist skin |
| 3. Cockroach | (c) Gills |
| 4. Fish | (d) Lungs and moist skin |
| 5. Earthworm | (e) Lungs |

**D. State whether the following statements are true (T) or false (F).**

1. The thick fur of polar bears keeps them warm in cold weather.
2. Snakes do not have legs.
3. All insects have wings.
4. Water boatman swims in water using its legs.
5. None of the birds migrate during the winter season.

**E. Give two examples for each of the following.**

1. Animals that live in oceans
2. Animals that live in forests
3. Animals that have shell as their body covering
4. Animals that breathe through spiracles
5. Reptiles that crawl using their short legs

**F. Give reasons for the following.**

1. Camels have thick eyelids.
2. The body of a Polar bear is covered with a thick fur.
3. Webbed feet are essential for water birds.
4. Salmon migrate to long distances.
5. The moist skin of earthworms is essential for their survival.

**G. Answer the following questions briefly.**

1. What are the different types of habitats found on the Earth?
2. What is blubber?
3. Define adaptation.
4. What is moulting?
5. How do aquatic animals, such as fish, breathe in water?

**H. Answer the following questions.**

1. Define habitat and write the main features of any two habitats.
2. Explain any three types of body coverings of animals with examples.
3. Describe any three types of breathing organs in animals with examples.
4. Write a note on the how aquatic animals and insects move.
5. Define migration. Why do animals migrate? Explain with examples.

# Cognitive Corner

## Critical Thinking

1. How is the movement of penguin different from that of other birds?
2. How is a whale different from a fish even though both are aquatic animals?
3. Why do birds migrate during winter?

## Picture Study

Look at the pictures given below. Circle the odd one, based on their body coverings.

## Project

Collect pictures of various animals from old newspapers and magazines. Group them according to their habitat and paste them in your scrapbook. Write a few lines about their adaptations in each habitat.

## Life Skills

Which of the following pictures show the correct way of treating animals/plants/habitat? Put a tick mark (✓) against the correct action and cross (✗) against the wrong action.

Planting a sapling ☐

Feeding a dog ☐

Boy throwing garbage in a pond ☐

# Worksheet

Life started on the Earth as plant-like organisms in the oceans. They then evolved into plants in water. Slowly microscopic animals were born. Life then shifted to land. The structure of all organisms changed over time. Over the time, they grew new structures, or shed the old ones to adapt to changes in the environment. This was done over a very, very long period of time and is called **adaptation**.

A. Which body part in a parrot and a bat help them to fly?

______________

B. As you know, the parrot is a bird, while the bat is a mammal. Select the method of adaptation they have used in order to fly.

Parrot

Bat

| Feathers | Long arms with finger bones |
|---|---|

Bat: ____________________ Parrot: ____________________

C. Why do you think adaption is important for life on land?

____________________________________________

____________________________________________

D. Collect pictures of any two animals found in different habitats on land and highlight the adaptations that help them to survive in those regions in the space provided below.

# 3 Skeletal System and Nervous System

## Learning Checklist

- Skeletal system
- Nervous system
- Sense organs

## Let's Get Started

Look at the pictures given below and fill in the blanks with the help of the words in the box.

| brain | muscles | bones |
|---|---|---|

I am able to run and stretch using the ____________ and ____________ in my body.

I am able to think and solve sums using my ____________ .

All the bones in our body are a part of the skeletal system. We use our brain to think, read, write, etc. The brain is part of our nervous system. In this chapter, we will learn more about the skeletal system and the nervous system.

# SKELETAL SYSTEM

a

The skeletal system consists of bones and cartilage. There are 206 bones in an adult human body. This framework of bones is called the **skeleton**, which gives support and shape to the body.

Following are some of the functions of the human skeletal system:

- It protects the soft internal organs of our body.
- It gives strength, support and shape to the body, and also helps in movement.
- It contains important minerals needed by our body.
- Many bones are hollow and filled with a substance called **bone marrow**. Bone marrow produces blood cells.

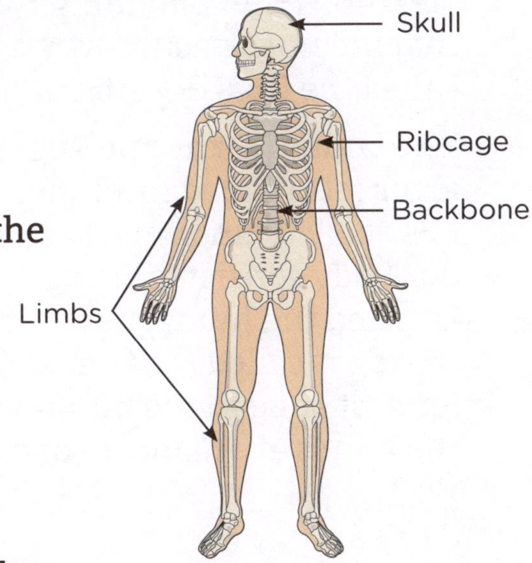

The human skeletal system

The main parts of the skeletal system are the skull, the backbone, the ribcage and the limbs.

**The Skull:** The hard structure that you feel when you touch and press your head is called the skull. It protects the brain. The skull has 22 bones. It also has holes where the eyes, nose and ears are positioned. Of all the bones in the skull, only the lower jawbone can move; all others are fixed. The upper and lower jaws have teeth.

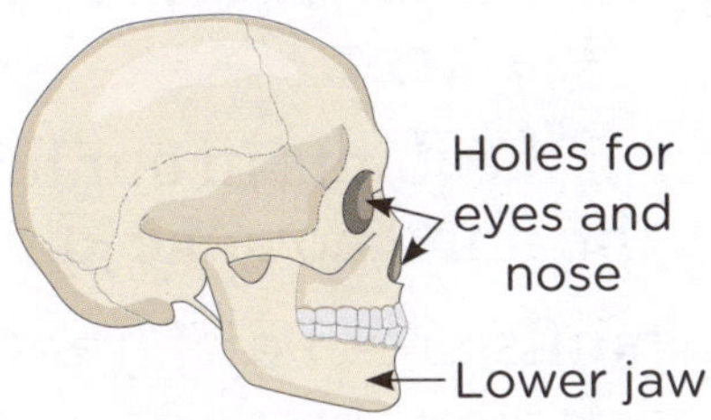

Skull

**The Backbone (Spine):** The long bone that you feel when you run your hand through the centre of your back is called the **backbone**, the spine, or the vertebral column. The backbone is made up of 33 small bones called the **vertebrae**. These bones help us in bending, twisting and turning. It also helps in keeping the body upright. The backbone protects the spinal cord inside it, which is connected to the brain in the skull.

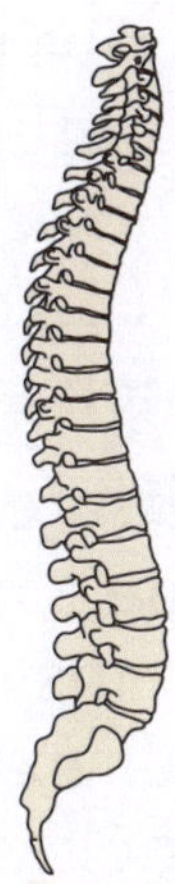
Backbone

**The Ribcage:** The frame of bones that forms a cage-like structure in the chest area is called the ribcage.

It protects the heart and the lungs. It is made up of 12 pairs of long curved bones called the **ribs**. These ribs join the backbone at the back. Ten pairs of ribs are joined to the front bone called the breastbone or **sternum**. The remaining two pairs of ribs that are not attached to the breastbone are called the **floating ribs**.

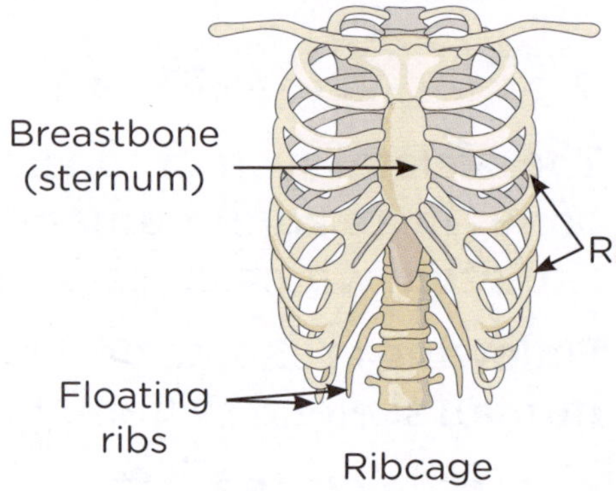

Ribcage

**The Limbs (Arms and Legs):** A pair of arms (also called forelimbs) and a pair of legs (also called hindlimbs) are what the limbs in our body consist of. The long bone in the arm is called the **humerus** and the thigh bone in the leg is called the **femur**. The femur is the longest bone in the human body. The feet and the hands are made up of many smaller bones.

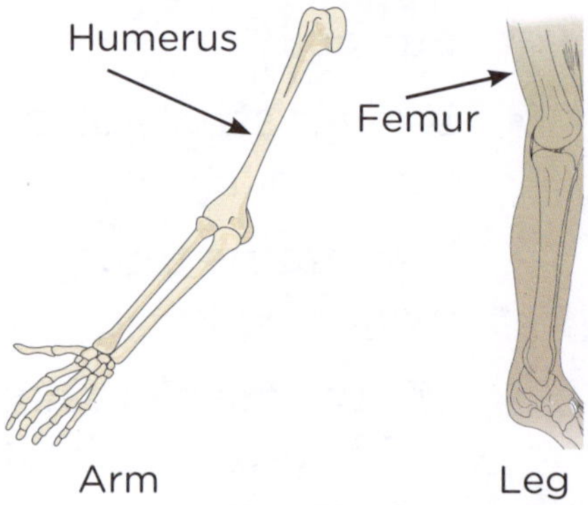

Limbs

## Joints

The place where two bones meet is called a **joint**. The substance or the tissue that joins two bones or holds together two bones in place is called a **ligament**.

All the joints in our body are movable except the joints in the skull. The only movable joint in the skull is the lower jaw.

Joints are of different types and show different kinds of movements:

**Ball and Socket Joint:** This type of joint is found in the **shoulder** and **hip** regions, and allows for the movement of these parts in all directions. This joint helps in movements such as bending, stretching and rotating.

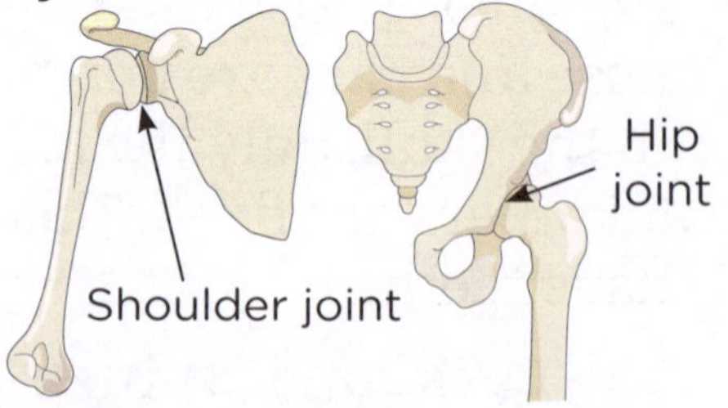

Ball and socket joints

**Hinge Joint:** This type of joint is found in the elbows, fingers, knees and toes, and helps us to move them in only one direction. For example, you can bend your lower leg backwards. You can bend your elbows and touch your shoulder with your hand.

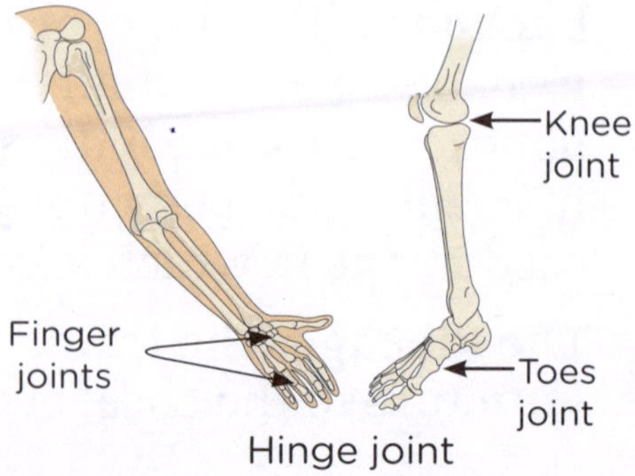

Hinge joint

**Pivot Joint:** This type of joint is found between the skull and the backbone, and helps us to move our head upwards, downwards and sideways.

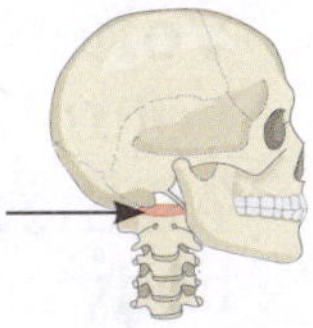


Pivot joint

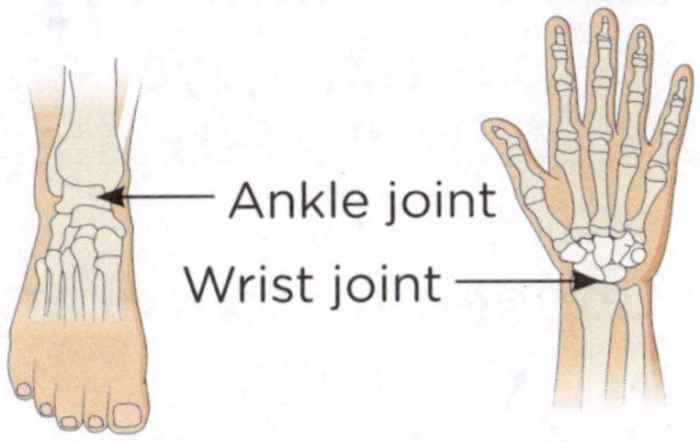


Gliding joints

**Gliding Joint:** This type of joint is present in the ankles and the wrists, and helps the bones of these parts to slide easily.

## Cartilage

Cartilage is a tough, elastic tissue that is found in various parts of the body, such as the joints in the ankle, knee and elbow, and also between the vertebrae in the backbone. Cartilage prevents bones from rubbing against each other and wearing out.

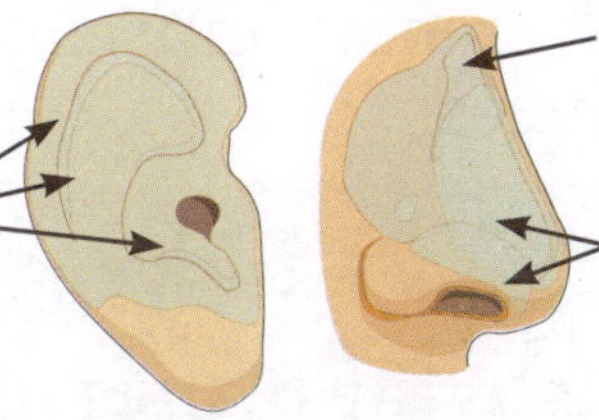


Cartilage in the ear and the nose

Cartilage is also found in the ears and the nose. Touch the top part of your ear or the tip of your nose. These parts are soft to touch. They are the cartilages.

Bones and cartilage alone cannot bring about movement. Movement happens when bones and cartilage work together with muscles.

Let us learn how bones and muscles work together.

### Science in Context

A baby's skeletal system is mostly made up of cartilage. As the baby grows, most of the cartilage is replaced by bones.

## Muscles

There are more than 600 muscles in our body. The bones in our body cannot move without the help of muscles. Muscles are attached to the bones with the help of tough cords called **tendons**. To move a bone, two muscles come into play. When you want to move your arm or leg, one muscle has to contract and another muscle has to relax to allow for the movement of the arm or the leg. **Muscles are of two types:** voluntary and involuntary.

**Voluntary Muscles:** The muscles that are under our control are called voluntary muscles.

All the muscles attached to the skeleton (called **skeletal muscles**) of the body are voluntary muscles, for example, the muscles in the arms and legs.

When looked through a microscope, these muscles seem to have bands or stripes on them. Therefore, they are also called **striped** or **striated muscles**.

**Involuntary Muscles:** The muscles that are not under our control are called involuntary muscles.

Muscles of the organ systems, such as the digestive system, are called **smooth muscles** or **unstriated muscles**, because they are not striped. Muscles of the heart are called **cardiac muscles**.

Both smooth muscles and cardiac muscles are examples of involuntary muscles.

## Revise and Recall

**Fill in the blanks using the words from the help box.**

600 Ten 206 33 Tendon

1. The skeletal system is made up of __________ bones.
2. There are about __________ muscles in our body.
3. __________ pairs of ribs are joined to the breastbone.
4. The backbone is made up of __________ small bones.
5. __________ is a tough cord that connects the muscle to the bone.

# NERVOUS SYSTEM

a

What helps you remember the topics that you have read in your previous chapters or classes?

How do you blink your eyes without even knowing about it?

We are able to do these tasks with the help of the nervous system.

The nervous system is made up of the brain, the spinal cord and a network of nerves that run throughout our body.

The nervous system controls all the other organ systems of our body.

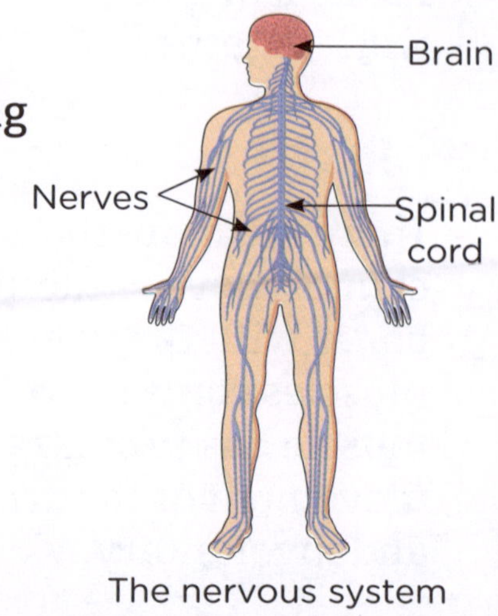

The nervous system

## Brain

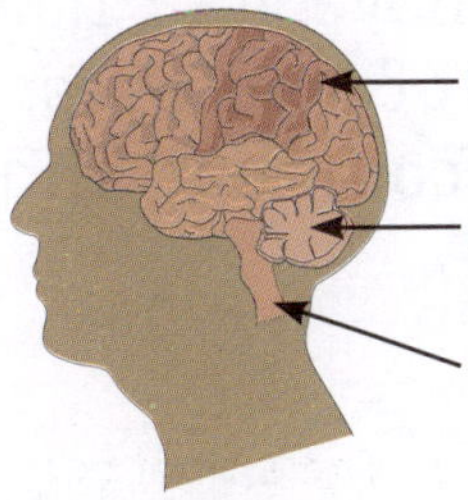

The human brain

The brain controls everything in the human body. The skull protects the brain. The part of the skull that protects the brain is called the **cranium**.

The brain is made up of three parts that carry out different tasks. They are the cerebrum, the cerebellum and the brainstem.

**Cerebrum:** This is the largest part of the brain. It controls our intelligence, memory, logic and sense organs. It also controls our body movements.

**Cerebellum:** This is the second largest part of the brain and is present behind the cerebrum. It controls the balance and posture of our body, and also the actions of the muscles in the body.

**Brainstem:** The brainstem connects the brain to the spinal cord. The nerves in the brainstem control our heartbeat, breathing and blood pressure.

**Science in Context**

The average adult human brain weighs about 1.3 to 1.4 kg.

## Spinal Cord

The spinal cord is a bunch of nerves that begins from the base of the brain and connects it to the other parts of the body.

It is enclosed and protected by the backbone. Its main function is to pass on information between the brain and the other body parts.

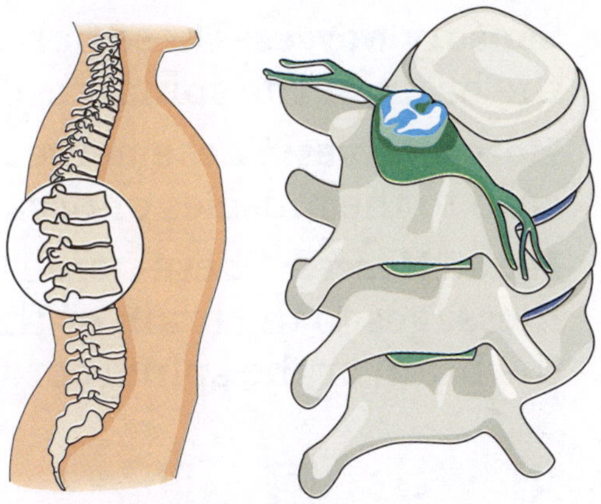
Spinal cord inside the backbone

## Reflex Actions

A reflex action is an involuntary or automatic action of our body in response to something.

Most reflex actions take place when the messages are sent to and from the spinal cord, without involving the brain. Hence, such responses are very fast.

For example, if you touch a hot object by mistake, a reflex causes you to remove your hand immediately. You blink when something flies in front of your eyes; you step back when someone tries to fall on you. Even coughing and sneezing are reflexes.

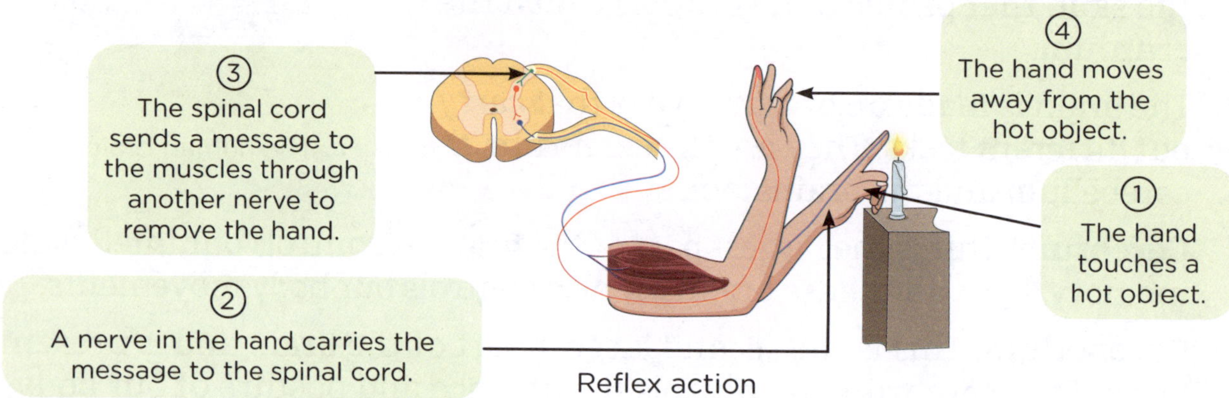


Reflex action

## Nerves

Nerves are bundles of long, thin, thread-like structures that carry messages between the brain or spinal cord and other parts of the body. Depending on their function, there are three main types of nerves in our body.

**Sensory Nerves:** These nerves carry messages from the sense organs to the brain or the spinal cord.

**Motor Nerves:** These nerves carry messages from the brain or spinal cord to the muscles or organs.

**Mixed Nerves:** These nerves carry out both the functions, that is, carry messages to the brain or the spinal cord and bring back messages from the brain or the spinal cord.

## SENSE ORGANS

Sense organs are the organs that give messages about our surroundings to our nervous system. The sense organs include the eyes, the ears, the nose, the tongue and the skin.

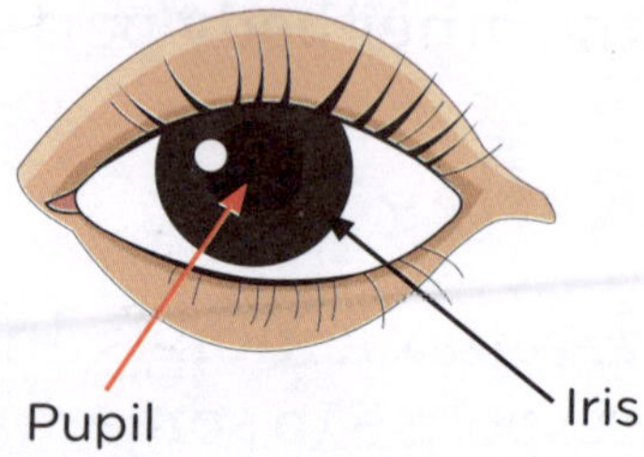


**Eyes:** We have two eyes to help us see. The coloured part of our eye is called the **iris**. The black circle in the centre of the eye is called the **pupil**, which allows light to enter through it.

A transparent, dome-shaped part, called the **cornea**, covers the front portion of the eye and protects the pupil and the iris. The lens is present behind the iris.

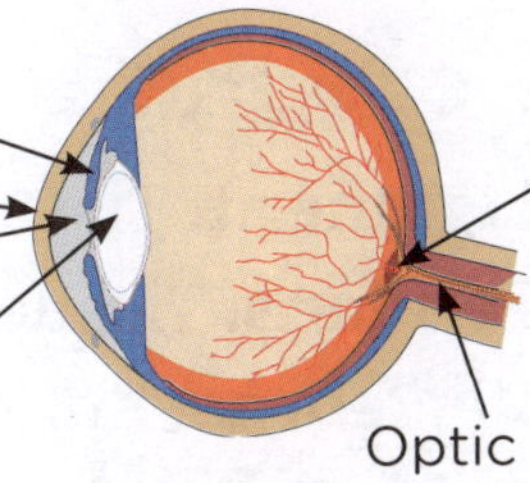

The human eye

The inner part of our eye has a very thin layer of tissues called the **retina** which captures the light that enters the eye and sends it to the brain through the **optic nerve**.

**Nose:** The nose helps us to smell and breathe. The nose has two holes called **nostrils**.

At the back of the nose, there is a space called the **nasal cavity**. It is separated from the mouth by a bony structure called the **palate**.

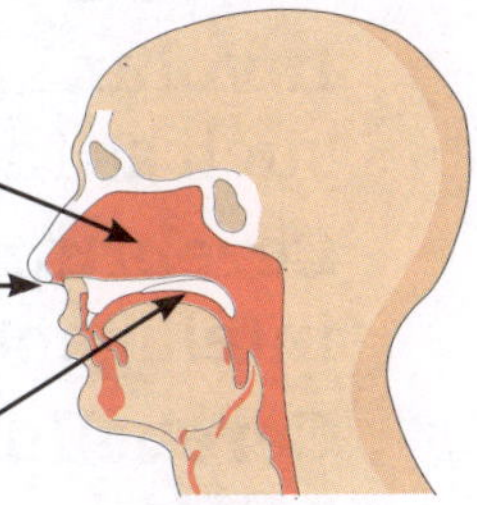

The nose

**Ears:** The ears help us to hear sounds. The outer part of the ear that we can see is called the **pinna**. It collects sound and sends it to the **eardrum**. The eardrum sends vibrations to the **inner ear** through the **middle ear**.

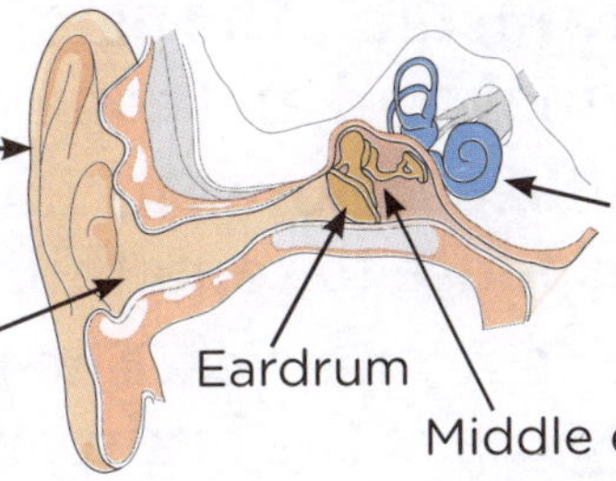

Parts of the ear

The inner ear converts these vibrations to a signal which is sent to the brain.

**Tongue:** The tongue is a fleshy sense organ found on the floor of the mouth. It helps us to speak, chew and taste.

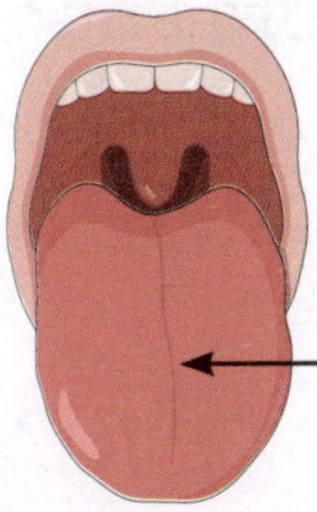


The taste buds on the tongue help us to identify the different tastes by sending signals to the brain.

The primary tastes that the tongue can sense are sweet, salty, sour, bitter and umami (or savoury; for example, the taste of meaty broth and fermented food).

**Skin:** The skin, which is the largest organ and the outer covering of the body, can sense touch and helps us to feel heat, cold, pain, etc.

The skin carries out many functions needed for our survival, which include wound healing, protection, maintaining the body temperature and preventing infections.

**Science in Context**

Butterflies can taste with their feet as they have taste sensors in their feet.

## Keywords

**Ligament:** Tissue that holds together two bones in place

**Tendons:** Tissues that help the muscles to attach to the bones

**Vertebrae:** Small bones that make up the backbone

**Voluntary muscles:** The muscles that are under our control, such as muscles in the arms and legs

**Involuntary muscles:** The muscles that are not under our control, such as the heart muscles

**Cerebrum:** The largest part of the brain that controls our intelligence, memory, logic and sense organs

**Cerebellum:** The second largest part of the brain that controls the balance and posture of our body, and also the actions of our muscles

**Brainstem:** The part of the brain that connects the brain to the spinal cord and controls our heartbeat, breathing and blood pressure

**Reflex action:** The involuntary or automatic action of our body in response to something

**Sensory nerves:** The nerves that carry messages from the sense organs to the brain or the spinal cord

**Mixed nerves:** The nerves that carry messages to the brain or spinal cord and also bring back messages from the brain or spinal cord

## Summary

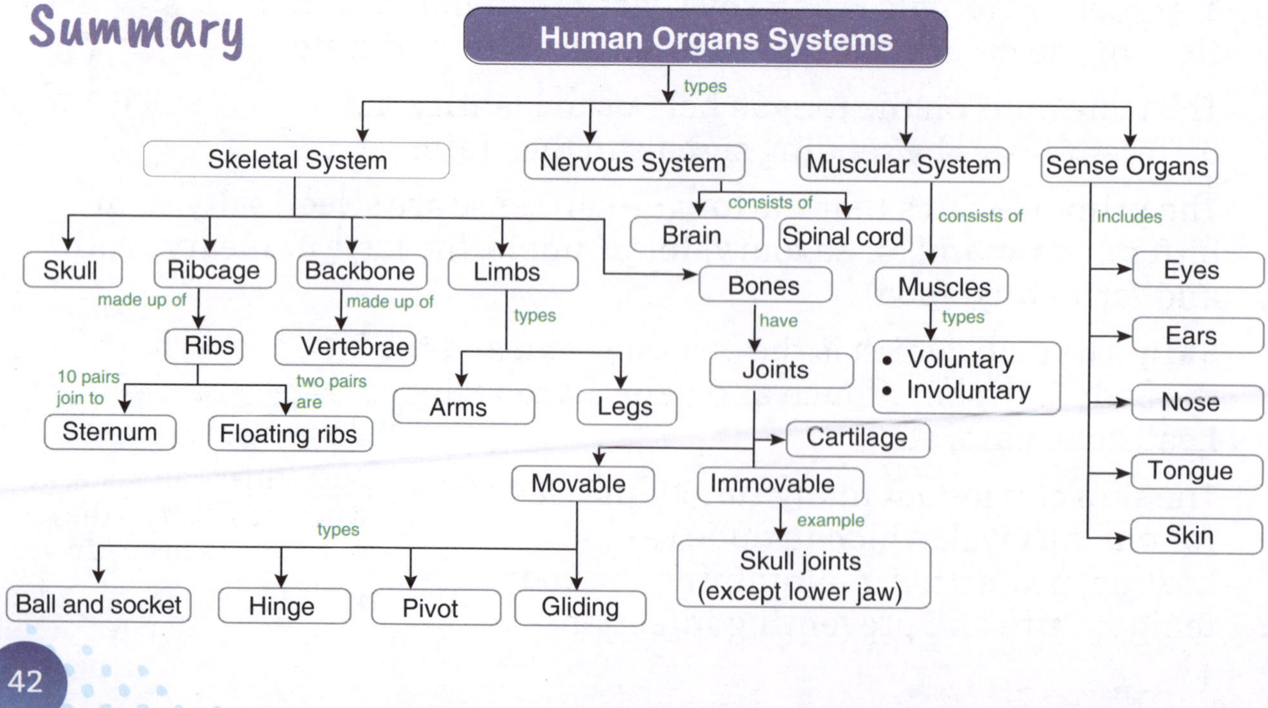

# Exercise

W

**A. Choose the correct option for each of the following.** ia

1. The function of the skeletal system is to give __________ to the body.
   (a) support (b) shape (c) strength (d) All of these
2. The joint between the skull and the backbone is __________.
   (a) ball and socket (b) pivot (c) hinge (d) gliding
3. Ten pairs of ribs are connected in the front to the __________.
   (a) backbone (b) sternum (c) brain (d) nerves
4. Which of these structures protects the brain?
   (a) Backbone (b) Ribcage (c) Skull (d) Forelimb
5. Most reflex actions are controlled by the __________.
   (a) brain (b) spinal cord (c) ribs (d) joints

**B. Fill in the blanks using the correct words.** ia

1. __________ protects the soft internal organs of our body. (Nerves/Skeleton)
2. The __________ controls everything that the body does. (brain/bones)
3. __________ muscles are attached to the skeleton. (Voluntary/ Involuntary)
4. Most of the joints in the skull are __________. (movable/immovable)
5. The nasal cavity is separated from the mouth by a bony structure called __________. (cranium/palate)

**C. Match the following.**

| Column A | Column B |
|---|---|
| 1. Humerus | (a) Hinge joint |
| 2. Ankle | (b) Tissue that joins two bones |
| 3. Hips | (c) Gliding joint |
| 4. Knees | (d) Ball and socket joint |
| 5. Ligament | (e) Long bone in the arm |

**D. State whether the following statements are true (T) or false (F).**

1. Bones and muscles work together to bring about movement.
2. Gliding joints are found between the small bones in the vertebral column.
3. The nervous system is made up of the brain, the heart and the nerves.

4. The brainstem controls our intelligence, memory, logic and sense organs.
5. The skin is the largest organ in our body.

**E. Name the following.**

1. The longest bone in the human body
2. A place where two bones meet
3. A type of joint in the shoulder
4. The system that controls everything you do
5. The part of the brain that helps us to maintain the balance of our body

**F. Give reasons for the following.**

1. Cartilage is found near joints.
2. Bones cannot move without the help of muscles.
3. The spinal cord connects the brain and other body parts.
4. A person with head injury often suffers from loss of memory.
5. Muscles are connected to motor nerve.

**G. Answer the following questions briefly.**

1. How many pairs of ribs are there in a human body? What are floating ribs?
2. What are joints? Name the different types of joints found in a human body.
3. What is cartilage? Where is it found in the body?
4. Name the three parts of the brain. Which is the largest part of the brain?
5. What is a reflex action?
6. Name the different types of nerves.

**H. Answer the following questions.**

1. What are the functions of the human skeletal system?
2. Name the main parts of the skeletal system. Explain the structure of the ribcage and the spinal cord.
3. Describe the two types of muscles in our body. Give examples for each.
4. What are the functions of the different parts of the brain?
5. Explain how a reflex action takes place when you touch a hot pan.
6. What are sense organs? Explain briefly the functions of each sense organ.

# Cognitive Corner

## Critical Thinking

1. What would happen if we injure our spinal cord critically?
2. Why do people find it difficult to move their body as they get older?

## Picture Study

Label the different parts of the brain in the following diagram.

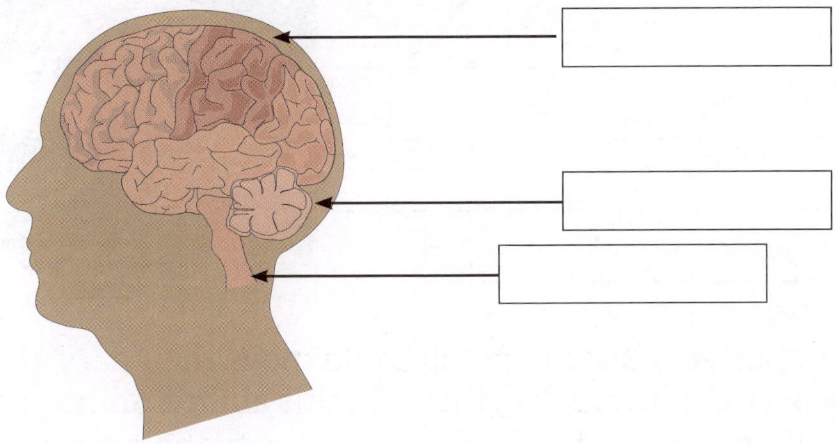

## Project

1. Prepare a chart about the different types of joints present in our body and display it in your class. Also, write the kind of movement shown by each joint.
2. Write a story in 100 words about a dish you made in the kitchen. Use the terms related to different tastes that the tongue can sense in your story.

## Life Skills

A diet that has food grains, vegetables, fruits, proteins and small amounts of milk and fats helps to keep our skeletal and nervous systems healthy.

Exercise and good sleep keep the brain active and the body fit. Exercises such as brisk walking, swimming, running, playing and dancing help to maintain a healthy body weight and make the bones stronger.

Write five healthy habits in your notebook that you will follow to keep your skeletal and nervous systems healthy.

# Worksheet

Man has evolved over centuries. Therefore, many parts of our body which were needed by our ancestors then are no longer needed by us now. *These organs, which once performed a function but now no longer have any use are called* ***vestigial organs***.

A. You might have seen a dog moving its ears. Why do you think it does so?

In the distant past, our ancestors too could move their ears. However, during long period of evolution, they lost this ability. Some people still have the ability to wiggle their ears. This is due to the presence of some vestigial ear muscles that allows wiggling of ears.

B. It is believed that ancient humans used to have a tail. Find more about it and write in the space given below.

C. Can you think of any more vestigial organs in human beings? Write about any one vestigial organ.

# 4 Food and Health

**Learning Checklist**

- Components of food
- Balanced diet
- Diseases

## Let's Get Started

We get food from both plants and animals. Look at the pictures of the food items given below and name the sources (plant or animal) from which these are obtained.

Eggs

______________

Rice

______________

Potato fries

______________

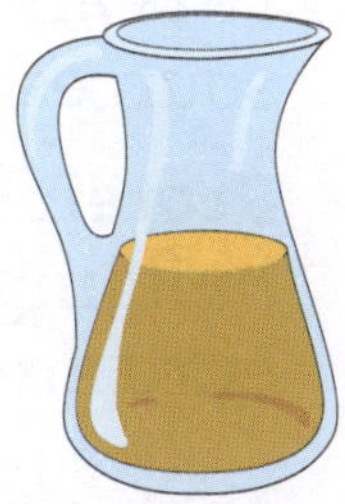
Orange juice

______________

Cheese

______________

Bread

______________

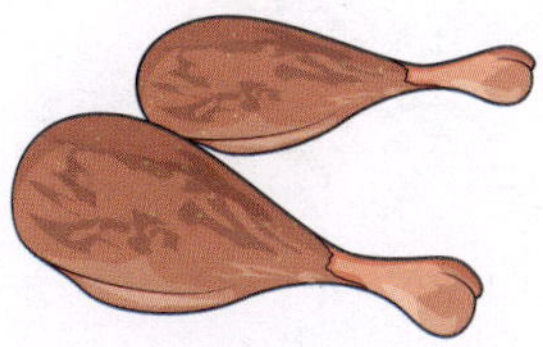
Chicken

______________

Ice cream

______________

Have you ever thought why you eat different varieties of food and not just your favourite food item all the time?

In this chapter, we will learn about the need to eat a variety of food, and the importance of rest and exercise in keeping us healthy and fit.

# COMPONENTS OF FOOD

Food contains nutrients[1] that are required by the body in adequate[2] amounts to grow and stay healthy. The main nutrients present in food are carbohydrates, fats, proteins, vitamins and minerals. Food also contains water and roughage.

**Word Web**

[1]**Nutrients:** components found in food that give strength and help the body to grow

[2]**Adequate:** sufficient in quantity

Carbohydrates, proteins and fats are called **macronutrients**, as these are required in large quantities in our daily diet, while vitamins and minerals are called **micronutrients**, as these are required in small quantities in our daily diet.

**Carbohydrates** are the main source of energy for our body. Rice, wheat, ripe fruits, bread, honey, sugar and potato are some food items rich in carbohydrates.

**Fats** also provide energy to the body. Butter, oil, ghee and nuts are rich sources of fats.

**Proteins** help in the growth and repair of tissues. They also help in building muscles. Groundnut, beans, pulses, fish, eggs, milk, cheese and curd are some food items rich in proteins.

Sources of carbohydrates

Sources of fats

Sources of proteins

Sources of vitamins

**Vitamins** are required in small amounts to keep our body fit and protect it against diseases. Green leafy vegetables, carrot and fruits are some food items rich in vitamins.

Sources of minerals

**Minerals** help in the physical and mental development of the body, and keep our bones and teeth strong and healthy. Milk, cheese, eggs, fruits and vegetables are some food items rich in minerals.

**Roughage** (also called dietary fibre) is the undigested portion of the plant food. It adds bulk to our diet. It helps in the easy passage of food through the digestive system. Cereals, unpolished rice and grains, fresh fruits and vegetables are some of the rich sources of roughage.

**Water** is required for almost all functions of the body. We should drink plenty of water (at least 8–10 glasses daily) to stay healthy.

## BALANCED DIET

A diet that has all the components of food in adequate amounts is called a **balanced diet**.

A balanced diet is essential for the proper growth and functioning of the body.

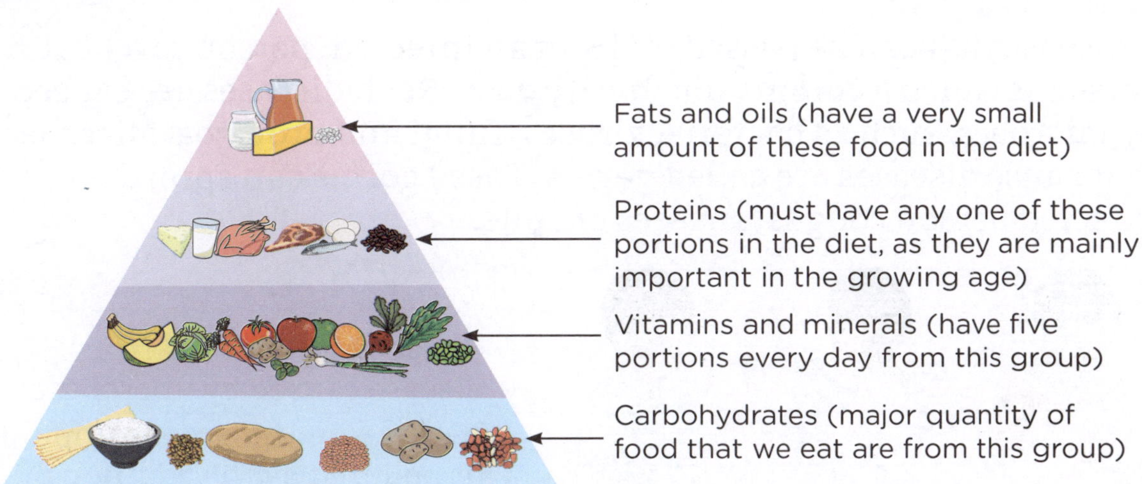


Diet pyramid

In addition to a balanced diet, our body needs regular exercise as well as adequate rest and sleep to stay healthy and active. Exercise keeps our bones and muscles strong. Rest and sleep keep us relaxed and refreshed.

## Revise and Recall

**Fill in the blanks using the correct words.**

1. Milk and milk products are rich in ______________ . (protein/fat)
2. ______________ protect our body from diseases. (Vitamins/Minerals)
3. Roughage is the ______________ portion of the plant food. (digested/undigested)
4. We should eat ______________ portions of fruits and vegetables every day. (two/five)

# DISEASES

a

**Health** is defined as a state of complete physical and mental well-being. A **disease** is a state where the body and/or mind are not in a healthy condition. A disease can occur due to many reasons. We can broadly classify diseases into two categories: communicable diseases and non-communicable diseases.

## Communicable Diseases

A disease that can be passed on from an infected[1] person to a healthy person is called a **communicable disease**. Such diseases are caused by microbes, such as bacteria, viruses, fungi and protozoa. Microbes that cause diseases are called **germs**. These germs can spread when the infected person coughs, sneezes or spits.

Coughing Sneezing Spitting

### Word Web

[1]**Infected:** suffering from a disease caused by microbes

[2]**Contaminated:** made impure or polluted by the addition of harmful substances or microbes

Germs can enter a person's body through contact with an infected person and/or contaminated[2] air, food or water. Insects, such as flies and mosquitoes, also spread disease-causing germs.

Prevention is better than cure. It is always better to prevent a disease than to treat it.

Cover your mouth while coughing and sneezing

Wash your hands before eating

Cover food and water

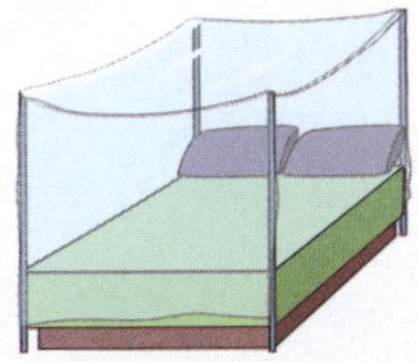

Use mosquito nets while sleeping

Maintaining good hygiene[1] and keeping the surroundings clean play a very important role in preventing diseases.

**Vaccination** is the process of using substances called vaccines[2] for the prevention of diseases. Many communicable diseases can be prevented by vaccinations given at the right time. Vaccination protects a person by not allowing the germs to multiply in case they enter the body.

**Word Web**

[1]**Hygiene:** to maintain cleanliness from germs and dirt

[2]**Vaccine:** a substance containing a very small amount of weakened germs that cause a disease. It is given to people to prevent them from getting that disease

[3]**Symptom:** sign of a particular disease

Some communicable diseases, their symptoms[3], and how they can be prevented or treated are given below.

| Communicable diseases | Caused by | Symptoms | Prevention/Cure |
|---|---|---|---|
| Flu | Virus | Sore throat, runny nose, difficulty in swallowing, fever, headache, cough and body ache | Take medicines, plenty of rest, plenty of fluids, cough drops, salt water gargling. |
| Measles | Virus | Runny nose, fever, cough, redness in the eyes, rashes, weight loss | Vaccination at an early age, plenty of fluids and bed rest can decrease the symptoms to some extent. |

| Communicable diseases | Caused by | Symptoms | Prevention/Cure |
|---|---|---|---|
| Chickenpox | Virus | Fever, headache, sore throat, tiredness, rashes that slowly dry up and then form scars | Vaccination at an early age, medicines, cool baths and bed rest. The rashes should not be scratched as they may spread to other parts on the body. |
| Cholera | Bacteria | Vomiting, dehydration, diarrhoea | Take medicines and plenty of fluids. |
| Malaria | Protozoa | Fever, chills, sweats, headaches, vomiting and body ache | Medicines to be taken on time, drips should be provided, use mosquito nets or mosquito-repellent cream, avoid storing water in open containers. |
| Typhoid | Bacteria | Headache, body ache, fever, diarrhoea | Take medicines and drips, boiled water, food without oil and spices, bed rest. |

**Science in Context**

Coronavirus disease, also called COIVD-19, is a highly infectious disease and has infected millions of people around the globe. This disease is caused by a new virus, the novel coronavirus. This virus can transmit from infected persons to healthy people through cough, sneeze and by contact. Hence, we should always cover our face and nose while coughing and sneezing and wash our hands properly with soap and water. We should also practice social distancing in public places.

## Non-communicable Diseases

A disease that cannot be passed on from one person to another is called a **non-communicable** disease.

Such diseases are mostly caused by the deficiency[1] of adequate amounts of nutrients in the diet. Hence, they are also called **deficiency disorders**.

**Word Web**

[1]**Deficiency:** lack of something

The following table gives some common deficiency disorders, their symptoms, together with the food that should be taken to prevent these diseases.

| Deficiency disorders | Symptoms | Food sources of that nutrient |
|---|---|---|
| Anaemia (iron deficiency) | Weakness, fatigue, difficulty in breathing | Raisins, apricots, milk, meat, apples, green leafy vegetables |
| Night blindness (vitamin A deficiency) | Inability to see in poor light or at night | Carrots, sweet potato, animal liver, red capsicum, lettuce |
| Beriberi (vitamin B1 deficiency) | Weight loss, weakness, low heartbeat, tiredness, affects growth of body and muscle formation | Beans, cereals, peas, fish, nuts, watermelon |
| Scurvy (vitamin C deficiency) | Irritation, swelling of joints, bleeding gums | Guavas, papaya, citrus fruits, tomatoes, grapes, berries |
| Rickets (vitamin D deficiency) | Softening and weakening of bones | Cod liver oil, fish, milk and dairy products, eggs, mushrooms, spinach |
| Goitre (iodine deficiency) | Difficulty in swallowing, tiredness, weight gain, swelling in the neck | Iodized salt, milk, boiled eggs, strawberries, yoghurt, baked potatoes |
| Kwashiorkor (protein deficiency) | Bloated belly, slow growth, change in skin and hair colour, weak development of limbs | Fish, eggs, meat, milk and other dairy products |

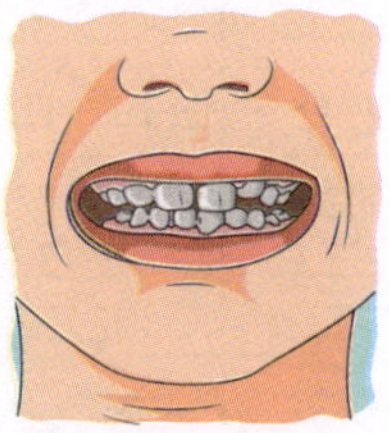

Vitamin C deficiency (Scurvy)

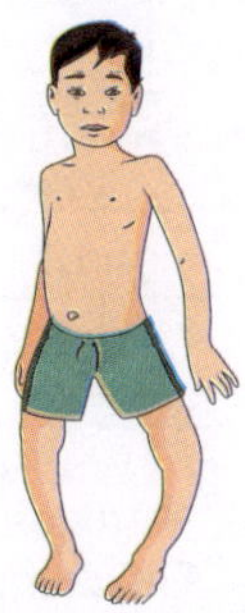

Vitamin D deficiency (Rickets)

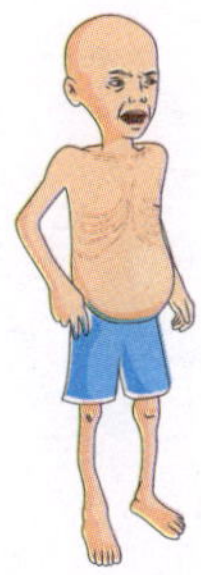

Protein deficiency (Kwashiorkor)

Iodine deficiency (Goitre)

## Keywords

**Macronutrients:** Nutrients required in large quantities in our daily diet

**Micronutrients:** Nutrients required in small quantities in our daily diet

**Roughage:** The undigested portion of plant food that adds bulk to our diet

**Communicable disease:** A disease that can be passed on from an infected person to a healthy person

**Non-communicable disease:** A disease that is not passed on from one person to another person

**Vaccination:** The process of using vaccines for the prevention of diseases

## Summary

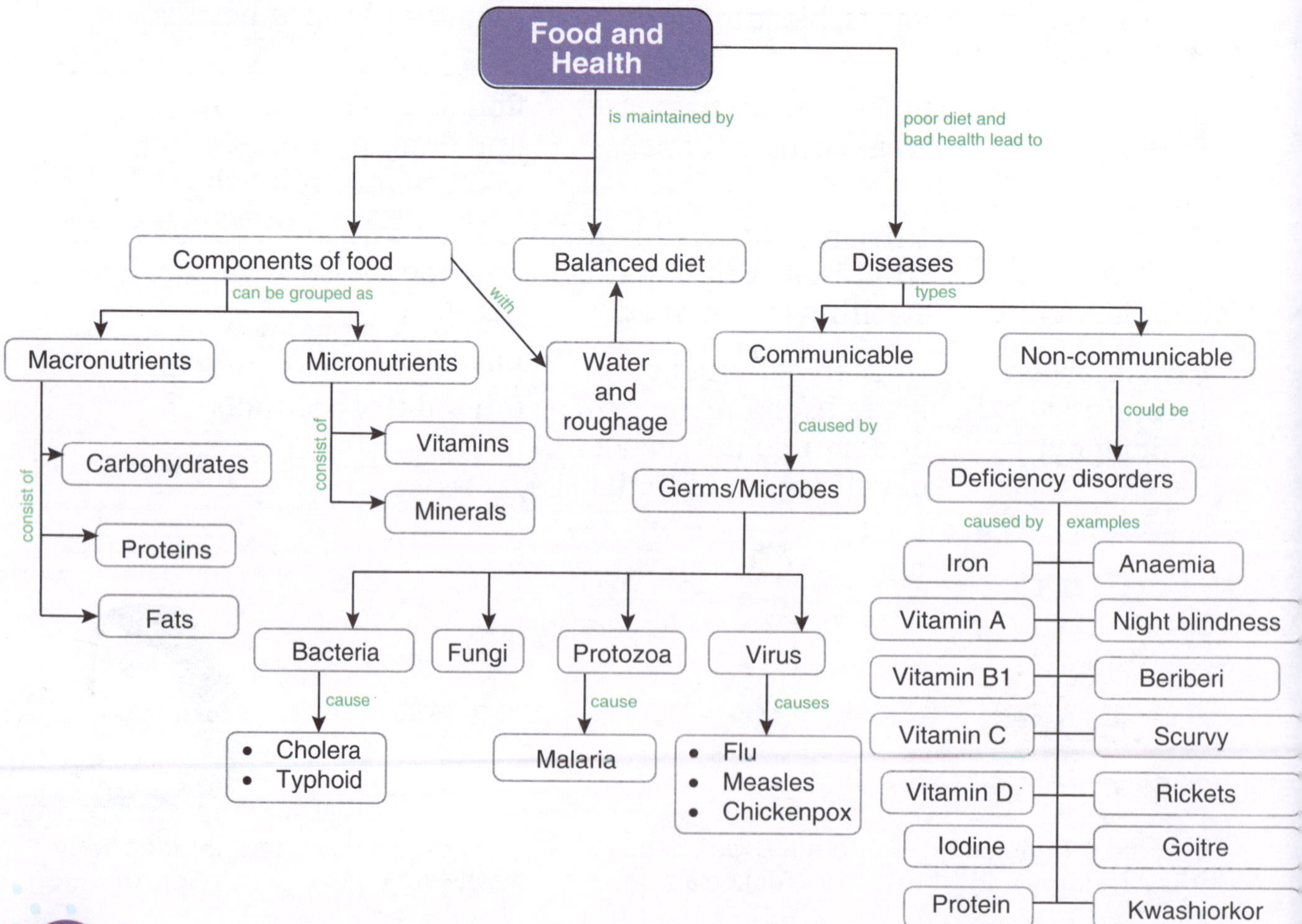

# Exercise

W

ia

**A. Choose the correct option for each of the following.**

1. Which of these are macronutrients?
   (a) Vitamins (b) Fats (c) Dietary fibres (d) Minerals
2. Food rich in ____________ keeps our bones and teeth strong.
   (a) fats (b) sugars (c) minerals (d) All of these
3. Which of the following is a communicable disease?
   (a) Typhoid (b) Malaria (c) Cholera (d) All of these
4. Vitamin B1 deficiency causes ____________.
   (a) weight loss (b) softening of bones
   (c) blindness (d) weight gain
5. Citrus fruits and tomatoes should be eaten to avoid ____________.
   (a) anaemia (b) night blindness (c) scurvy (d) goitre

**B. Fill in the blanks using the correct words.**

1. Nutrients required in small quantities in our daily diet are called ____________. (micronutrients/macronutrients)
2. ____________ are required for the physical and mental development of the body. (Vitamins/Minerals)
3. We should drink at least ____________ glasses of water daily. (1–3/8–10)
4. Non-communicable diseases can be avoided by following a good ____________. (diet/hygiene)
5. Vomiting and dehydration are the symptoms of ____________. (cholera/chickenpox)

**C. Match the following.**

| Column A | Column B |
|---|---|
| 1. Iodine deficiency | (a) Scurvy |
| 2. Vitamin C deficiency | (b) Goitre |
| 3. Vitamin B1 deficiency | (c) Anaemia |
| 4. Iron deficiency | (d) Rickets |
| 5. Vitamin D deficiency | (e) Beriberi |

**D. State whether the following statements are true (T) or false (F).**

ia

1. Proteins are the building materials of our body.
2. Vaccination can prevent communicable diseases.
3. Viruses and fungi cause non-communicable diseases.
4. We can have a balanced diet when we eat a variety of food in adequate amounts.
5. Plenty of fluids and bed rest can decrease the symptoms of measles to some extent.

**E. Give two examples for each of the following.**

1. Sources of carbohydrates
2. Sources of fats
3. Sources of vitamins
4. Sources of minerals
5. Sources of roughage

**F. Give reasons for the following.**

1. We must cover our mouth while coughing or sneezing.
2. Deficiency disorders are called non-communicable diseases.
3. We must include roughage in our diet.
4. Some people suffer from swelling of joints and bleeding of gums.
5. Vaccination taken at the right age will prevent communicable diseases.

**G. Answer the following questions briefly.**

1. What is roughage?
2. Give any two habits that should be followed to prevent communicable diseases.
3. Name two communicable and non-communicable diseases.
4. Why is exercise important?
5. What are the symptoms of night blindness?

**H. Answer the following questions.**

1. What are the different components of food? Also mention their important sources.
2. What are micronutrients and macronutrients? On what basis are they grouped?
3. What is a balanced diet? Why are water and roughage important in a balanced diet, even when they do not contain any nutrients?

4. What are communicable diseases? What are the symptoms of malaria and how can it be prevented?
5. What are deficiency disorders? What are the symptoms of rickets and how can it be prevented?

# Cognitive Corner

## Critical Thinking

1. How can a person with a cold or flu avoid spreading germs?
2. If you have eaten a lot of junk food and sweets, how would you compensate for it in your other meals for that day?
3. Manav mostly has a good diet but still feels lazy and gets tired easily. He does not exercise or play any outdoor games. He spends his weekends watching television or playing computer games. He often goes to bed late at night. What should Manav do to be active and fit?

## Picture Study

Identify the nutrients present in the food items given below.

______________

______________

______________

## Project

Make a food diary. List all the five nutrients in your diet that you will eat on one particular day. Jot down the portions of each food item you would have eaten for that day and present it to your class.

Ask your teacher to check your food diary and advise if you are following the right diet.

## Life Skills

Find out the food items eaten by your family members for a day and represent the data in a pie chart. Fill different parts of the pie chart with different colours. Find out if it is a balanced diet, and, if not, advise them on the benefits of eating a balanced diet.

# Worksheet

Have you ever seen flies rubbing their legs together? They rub their legs together to clean their feet and be able to sense their surroundings better.

Flies sit on anywhere, the garbage, animal excreta and so on; and in the process disease-causing germs stick to their bodies. When these flies sit on the food, they transfer the germs to the food by rubbing their legs. Through this contaminated food, the germs are transferred into our body, making us sick. Cholera and typhoid are some diseases that are spread by flies.

A housefly sitting on food

Make a colourful poster in the space provided below to spread awareness on how flies spread germs and make people sick. Also, suggest some of the measures that can be taken to prevent this.

# 5 Safety and First Aid

**Learning Checklist**

- Safety from fire
- First aid

## Let's Get Started

Look at the pictures given alongside and tick (✔) the correct answer for the given questions.

1. What should you do while lighting firecrackers?
   - You should light the firecrackers on your own. ☐
   - You should wear only synthetic clothes while lighting crackers. ☐
   - You should light the firecrackers only in the presence of an adult. ☐

2. How do you cross the road?
   - Before crossing, first look to your right, then to your left, and make sure that all the vehicles have stopped. Then cross the road. ☐
   - Always run while crossing the road so that you can reach the other end fast. ☐
   - As soon as you find a zebra crossing, run towards the other end without waiting for the signal. ☐

Accident

Accidents occur due to carelessness, when people do not follow safety rules. It is important to follow safety rules everywhere to avoid accidents.

You have learned in your previous classes about the safety rules to be followed at home, in school, on the road and in playground.

Let us now learn how to be safe from fire and the first aid that should be given for burns, animal bites, nosebleed, etc.

## SAFETY FROM FIRE

a

A fire can be caused due to any of the following reasons:

- Carelessness while handling burning matchsticks and candles is one of the main causes for fire accidents.
- Carelessness while burning firecrackers is also a major cause of fire accidents during festivals.
- Electrical faults can cause fire outbursts.
- Carelessness during cooking and gas leaks in the kitchen can also cause fire.

Lighting firecrackers in the presence of an elder

To prevent fire accidents, we must follow some safety rules:

- We should be very careful while handling fire. Children must never play with matchsticks or candle flame.
- Electrical appliances and wiring should be checked regularly for faults or wear and tear.
- Electrical faults should be fixed immediately.
- We should not wear nylon or synthetic clothes while cooking as they catch fire easily. Cotton or woollen clothes are safer.
- In case of a gas leak, open all doors and windows immediately. Do not strike a matchstick or handle any electric switch. Electric switches produce sparks when switched on or off. This may cause fire when it comes in contact with gas.
- Faulty gas pipes should be replaced.

Checking electrical appliances

## Putting Out Fire

We can put out a fire in the following ways:

Firefighter putting out fire

- Fire may spread very quickly. You know that fire needs air to keep burning. One method of putting out fire is to cut off the air supply. This can be done by throwing mud or sand over the fire.
- In case of a major fire, inform the nearest fire station. Firefighters put out fire with the help of a fire engine. A small fire can be put out using a special instrument called the **fire extinguisher**.
- In case your clothes or someone else's clothes catch fire, do not run around. This will fan the flames and make them spread. Stop where you are; drop to the ground and roll on the ground with your hands covering your face. Rolling puts off your flames. You can also use water to put out the fire or wrap yourself with a thick blanket or rug. But, do not stay covered with a blanket for too long.

### Revise and Recall

**Circle the words that are related to fire.**

Matches, campfire, pedestrian crossing, stove, traffic signal, bonfire, candles, smoke, crackers, knife, lighter, flame and sparks

# FIRST AID

When a person gets injured, a doctor or a nurse may not be available at that particular place and time. In such cases, the injured person should be given first aid immediately. **First aid** is the first or immediate help given to an injured person before he or she is taken to a doctor.

## First Aid for Cuts

Any cut or open wound on the skin should not be left unattended, as germs can enter our body through them. Wash the cut with clean water. Wipe it and apply an antiseptic cream or lotion. If there is loss of blood, tie a clean cloth or use a band-aid over the cut. One must go to a doctor in case of deep cuts.

## First Aid for Burns

In case of minor burns, keep the burnt area under cold running water for sometime, or apply ice cubes immediately. This will cool the burnt area. Then, apply an antiseptic cream on that area.

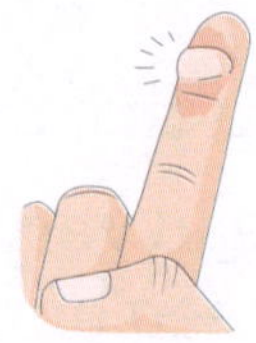
Blister

Cooling the burnt hand under cold running water

If the burn forms blisters[1], never try to prick them. Cover them with a soft cotton cloth. In case of severe burns, visit the nearest available doctor immediately.

### Science in Context

A solution of baking soda in water can be applied to the burnt area to get relief from the burning sensation.

### Word Web

[1]**Blister:** a small bubble-like swelling on the skin filled with water

[2]**Sling:** a strap or cloth that is tied around the neck to support a broken arm

[3]**Splint:** a piece of hard material (wood or cardboard) used to hold a broken bone in place

## First Aid for Fracture

A break or crack in the bone is called a **fracture**. When a bone gets fractured, there will be pain and swelling around the injured area. Ensure that the fractured part is not moved. For example, if there is a fracture in the arm, a cloth sling[2] made from a triangular piece of cloth can be used to support the arm. A splint[3] can also be used to give support to the broken bone. The injured person should be taken to the nearby hospital immediately.

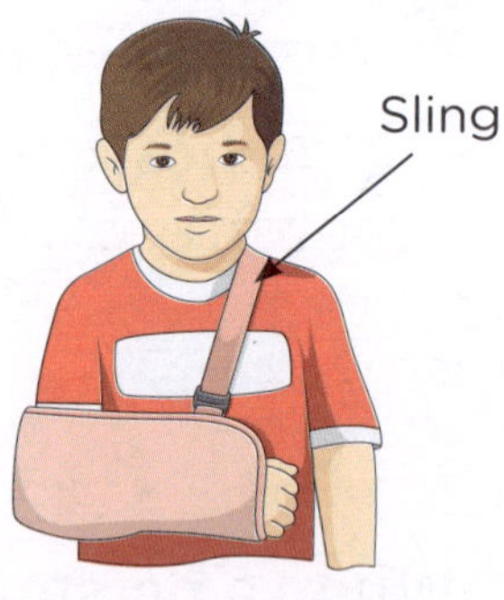

A sling for a fractured arm

Sometimes, the ankle or wrist can get twisted and cause pain. This is called a **sprain**. We should not move the sprained part. An elastic bandage can be wrapped around the sprained part.

## First Aid for Animal Bite

The bites of stray animals, such as dogs, cats and monkeys, can cause a disease called **rabies**. When these animals bite someone, they release saliva, containing germs, from their mouth.

The saliva enters the victim's[1] body through the wound and causes rabies. So, in case of an animal bite, the wound should be washed with soap under running water. An antiseptic cream should be applied and the wound should be covered with a clean bandage. The victim should be taken to the nearby doctor immediately.

**Word Web**

[1]**Victim:** a person who has been attacked or injured

**Science in Context**

It is important to identify the animal that bit a person, so that the nurse or doctor can treat the patient for its relative diseases, if necessary.

## First Aid for Snakebite

Snakes mostly hide in bushes. We need to be careful while playing in a garden near wild bushes. If a person is bitten by a venomous snake, the venom enters in the victim's body. The venom mixes with blood and spreads quickly in the body. In case of a snakebite, the following first aid should be given:

- A tight bandage should be tied just above the wound so that the spread of venom in the body may slow down.
- The victim should be kept calm and taken to the nearest available doctor immediately.

## First Aid for Insect Sting

Sometimes, we may get stung by insects, such as a bee or a wasp. In such cases, the sting should be removed first, and then, some ice cubes should be placed on the bitten area. An antiseptic cream can also be applied on this area.

For bee stings, a paste of baking soda or toothpaste can be applied. For wasp stings, lemon juice or vinegar can be applied.

## First Aid for Nosebleed

One may have nosebleeds in hot weather. In such cases, one should sit upright comfortably on a chair and lean forward slightly. The nose should be wiped with a clean handkerchief. Then, the index finger and thumb should be used to pinch the nose. The person should breathe through the mouth and not through the nose.

First aid for nosebleed

If the nosebleed does not stop, the person should be taken to a doctor.

## Keywords

**First aid:** The first or immediate help given to an injured person before he or she is taken to a doctor

**Fracture:** A break or crack in a bone

**Sprain:** An injury by a sudden twisting of joints that causes swelling and pain

**Rabies:** A disease caused by animal bites

## Summary

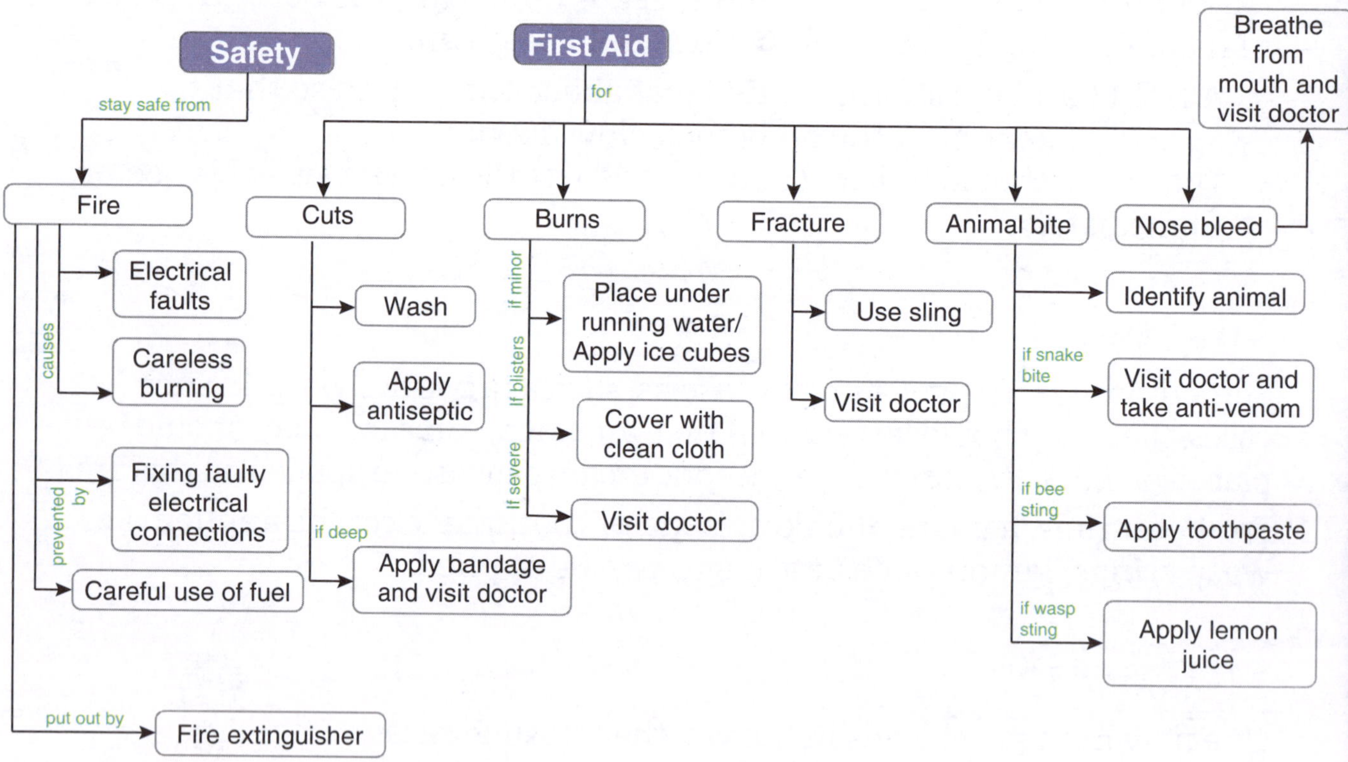

## Exercise

**A. Choose the correct option for each of the following.**

1. Fire needs ____________ to keep burning.
   (a) air (b) water (c) smoke (d) light
2. Nylon or synthetic clothes should not be worn while bursting firecrackers or while ____________.
   (a) going out (b) sitting (c) cooking (d) playing
3. In case of minor burns, keep the burnt area under ____________.
   (a) hot water (b) cold running water
   (c) boiling water (d) salt solution
4. Rabies is caused by ____________.
   (a) snakebites (b) animal bites (c) gas leak (d) fracture

**B. Fill in the blanks using the correct words.**

1. ____________ can cause fire outbursts. (Fire engines/Electrical faults)
2. A small fire can be put out using a fire ____________. (engine/extinguisher)
3. ____________ clothes do not catch fire easily. (Cotton/Nylon)

**C. Match the following.**

| Column A | Column B |
|---|---|
| 1. Band-aid | (a) Burns |
| 2. Blisters | (b) For fracture |
| 3. Splint | (c) For cuts |
| 4. Ice cubes | (d) Cool the burnt area |

**D. Name the following.**

1. Mud or sand is thrown over it to put it out
2. Instrument used by firefighters to put out fire
3. A cloth that is tied around the neck to support a broken arm
4. A disease that can be caused by an animal bite
5. A person who has been attacked or injured

**E. Give reasons for the following.**

1. First aid can be given at home for wasp stings.
2. A person whose nose is bleeding should breathe through the mouth.
3. A stray dog's bite victim should consult a doctor.

4. An elastic bandage can help a sprain, but not a fracture.
5. A tight bandage must be tied above a snake bite wound.

**F. Answer the following questions briefly.**

1. How are fires caused?
2. What should be done in case of a gas leak?
3. What is a fire extinguisher?
4. What first aid should be given for a fracture?
5. What is a sprain? What first aid should be given for a sprain?

**G. Answer the following questions.**

1. Write any three safety rules that should be followed to prevent fire accidents.
2. Write the various methods of putting out a fire.
3. Define first aid. What first aid can be given in case of burns?
4. What first aid can be given to a victim in case of an animal bite?

# Cognitive Corner

## Critical Thinking

1. You are playing with your friend in a garden. Suddenly, your friend gets stung by a bee. What will you do?
2. A person whose clothes catch fire should not run around. Why?

## Picture Study

Observe the pictures given below and write the type of accidents/ injury shown in each.

1. 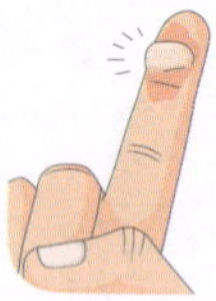

2. 

3. 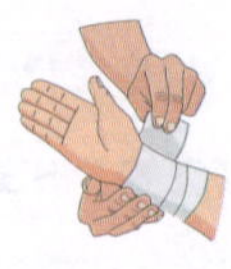

## Project

Fumy is the mascot for a campaign on fire safety. Join him for the campaign by making a poster on a few tips on safety from fire.

## Life Skills

Whom would you call if there is an emergency? Write down the phone numbers of the following emergency contacts.

1. Police
2. Ambulance
3. Fire station

# Worksheet

Our mouth and nose meet at the same entrance at the back of our throat. There is a flap called **epiglottis** which acts like a door. When we breathe in and out, it closes the entrance to our food pipe. When we swallow food or drink, it closes the passage that leads to our lungs.

Sometimes, when we are not careful, food or liquid enters the windpipe. Then we have a coughing fit till the food or liquid is thrown out. In case the food particle is big enough to block the windpipe, we will not be able to breathe. This dangerous situation is called choking. Thus, we should not talk or laugh while eating as it can make food go down the wrong way and result in choking.

A. What are the situations that can lead to choking? Tick (✓) the correct options and cross (✗) the incorrect ones.

Playing with food ☐

Eating properly ☐

Eating food in big chunks ☐

B. Write down the names of five things that you see your friends putting in their mouths that may lead to choking.

____________, ____________, ____________, ____________, ____________

C. Rahul has a younger sister who always plays with food and never eats it properly. How should Rahul explain to his sister about the bad effects of not paying attention to food while eating?

________________________________________

________________________________________

________________________________________

________________________________________

# 6 Air and Water

## Learning Checklist

- Layers of the atmosphere
- Composition of air
- Properties of air
- Water
- Purification of drinking water

## Let's Get Started

Rekha and Smita are sisters. They made a plan to celebrate their grandfather's birthday and bought balloons to decorate the house.

Look at the pictures and answer the question given below each.

What is Rekha blowing into the balloon?

______________________

Why did Smita's balloon burst?

______________________

Air and water are two of our basic necessities. In this chapter, we will learn about the composition and properties of air, and the ways to purify water.

# LAYERS OF THE ATMOSPHERE

a

The Earth is surrounded by a thick envelope of air called the **atmosphere**. In order to study the atmosphere, scientists have divided it into six layers.

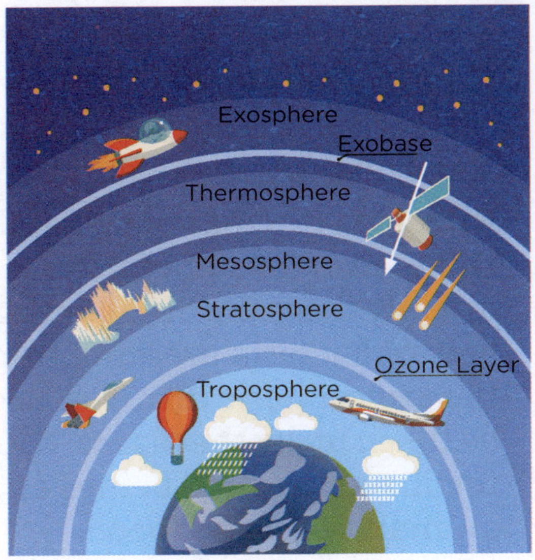


Layers of the atmosphere (not to scale)

**Troposphere**: This is the first layer of the atmosphere, just above the ground. Troposphere is where we live in and where most aeroplanes fly. The weather changes take place in this layer.

**Stratosphere:** This is the second layer of the atmosphere. The ozone layer is a part of the stratosphere. This layer absorbs harmful radiations from the sun and stops them from reaching the Earth's surface.

Jet planes fly in the stratosphere.

**Mesosphere:** This is the third layer of the atmosphere from the Earth's surface. This is the coldest among all the atmospheric layers.

Meteors[1] burn up in this layer while entering the Earth's surface. From the Earth, we see them as shooting stars.

**Word Web**

[1]**Meteors:** rocks from outer space that enter the Earth's atmosphere

**Thermosphere:** This is the fourth layer of the atmosphere from the Earth's surface. Space shuttles fly in this layer.

**Exosphere:** This is the uppermost layer of the atmosphere. There is no air beyond this. The air is very thin here.

**Ionosphere:** This layer overlaps the mesosphere, thermosphere and the exosphere. It changes its size depending on the energy it absorbs from the sun. This layer helps in radio communication.

The atmosphere is useful to us in many ways:

- It contains oxygen, which is essential for the survival of living things. It also contains carbon dioxide, which is required for photosynthesis.
- It helps to maintain the right temperature for the survival of living things.
- It has the ozone layer, which protects us from the harmful rays of the sun.

# COMPOSITION OF AIR

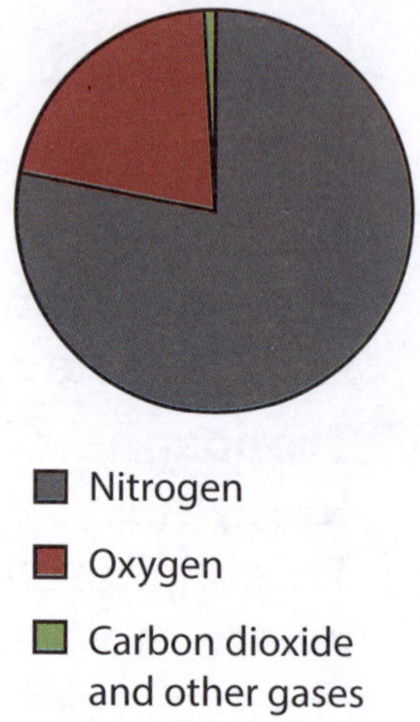


Air is a mixture of gases. It mainly consists of nitrogen (78%), oxygen (21%) and other components, such as carbon dioxide and other gases (1%). Air also contains small quantities of water vapour, dust and smoke.

**Nitrogen:** It is the most abundant gas in the atmosphere. Living things require nitrogen, but it cannot be taken directly from the air. Plants get nitrogen with the help of bacteria present in the soil. These bacteria fix the atmospheric nitrogen to different forms that can be taken up by the plants. Nitrogen is also added to the soil by means of fertilizers. Human beings and animals get nitrogen from both plant and animal sources of food.

**Oxygen:** Oxygen is necessary for the survival of living things. All living things need oxygen to breathe. Oxygen is also needed for burning. Green plants give out oxygen during the process of photosynthesis.

**Carbon dioxide and other gases:** Carbon dioxide is released into the atmosphere during breathing and burning. Plants use carbon dioxide for the process of photosynthesis. Other gases, such as helium, neon, hydrogen, argon, krypton and ozone, are also present in the air.

**Water vapour, dust and smoke:** Air also contains a small amount of water vapour, dust and smoke. Heat from the sun causes water to evaporate from the surface of the seas, oceans, lakes, etc. The amount of water present in the air is called **humidity**. It plays an important role in determining weather conditions.

## Activity 1

**Aim:** To show that oxygen is necessary for burning
**Materials required:** Two candles and a glass jar
**Procedure:**

1. Place the candles on a table and light them.
2. After a while invert the glass jar over one of the candles.

**Observation:** The candle that is exposed to air continues to burn, whereas the candle covered by the jar burns for a short while and then stops burning.
**Reason:** The flame of the candle in the jar goes off because covering the candle cuts off the oxygen supply.
**Conclusion:** This shows that oxygen is essential for burning.

Air is used in burning and breathing. Air also causes **rusting**. Objects made of iron get covered with a reddish brown substance called **rust**. This happens when iron objects come in contact with the oxygen and water vapour present in the air and form iron oxide. Iron objects such as gates and grills are painted to prevent exposure to air.

## PROPERTIES OF AIR

Air is matter, as it occupies space and has weight. Let us do these simple activities to understand these properties of air.

### Activity 2

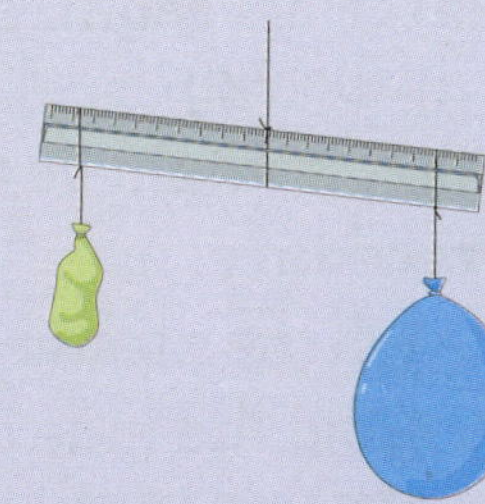

**Aim:** To show that air has weight

**Materials required:** Two balloons, a needle, two pieces of thread and a scale

**Procedure:**

1. Blow air into both the balloons.
2. Tie the balloons with the help of threads to either side of the scale.
3. Tie a thread to the middle of the scale and suspend it from a stand. Observe how the scale is positioned.
4. Now, burst one of the balloons with a needle.
5. Observe what happens.

**Observation:** When one of the balloons is burst, the scale tilts towards the balloon that has air.

**Reason:** This happens because the intact balloon has air inside it, which makes it heavier. Hence, the scale tilts.

**Conclusion:** Air has weight.

### Activity 3

**Aim:** To show that air occupies space

**Material required:** A balloon

**Procedure**:

1. Bring the balloon to your mouth and blow air in it.
2. Observe what happens.

**Observation:** The balloon increases in size when you blow air in it.

**Reason:** The air we blow into the balloon occupies space. Hence, the balloon increases in size.

**Conclusion:** Air occupies space.

As air occupies space, we are able to fill it in tyres, football bladders, swimming floats (life buoys, lifesaver or lifebelt) and air pillows.

Because of its weight, air pushes everything around it in all the directions. In other words, we say that air exerts **pressure**. This pressure is called the **air pressure**. Air pressure is greater near the surface of the Earth and lesser as we go up.

## Activity 4

**Aim:** To show that air exerts pressure

**Materials required:** Plastic cup and index card (cardboard)

**Note:** It might be a good idea to try this over a sink.

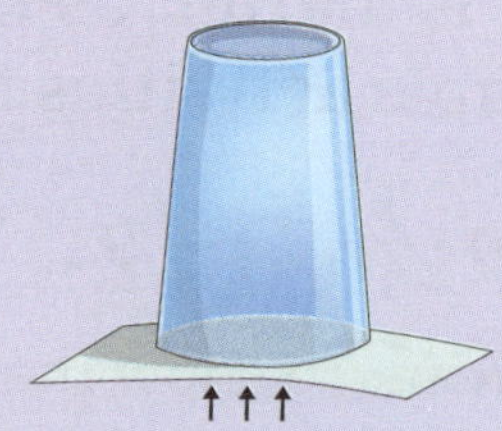

**Procedure:**

1. Fill the plastic cup with water. Place the index card on top of the cup.
2. Hold the index card tightly against the mouth of the plastic cup and turn the cup upside down.
3. Carefully remove your hand, holding the index card in place.

**Observation:** The index card does not fall.

**Reason:** The pressure of air outside the plastic cup is pushing the card up.

**Conclusion:** This shows that air exerts pressure on objects.

Not just upwards, air exerts pressure on all sides. When a balloon is blown over its maximum size, the air pressure increases. At some point, the air exerts too much pressure on the walls of the balloon and it bursts.

Some applications of air pressure in everyday life are given below.

Drinking through a straw

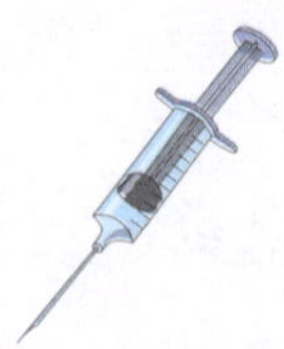

Filling up injection syringes

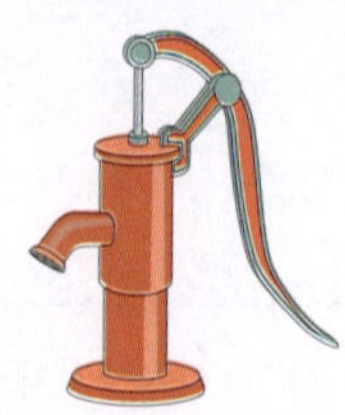

Getting water from a hand pump

Using a vacuum cleaner

Working of aeroplanes and sailboats

## Revise and Recall

**Fill in the blanks using the correct words.**

1. ______________ is added to the soil by the means of fertilizers. (Nitrogen/Argon)
2. All living things need ______________ to breathe. (oxygen/nitrogen)
3. The layer of atmosphere where weather changes take place is ______________. (troposphere/stratosphere)
4. Space shuttles fly in ______________. (exosphere/thermosphere)
5. Air exerts ______________ on objects. (weight/pressure)

# WATER

Like air, water is also essential for the survival of living things. We need water for drinking, cooking, bathing, etc. It is very important that we drink clean and pure water.

Rainwater, rivers, ponds, lakes and wells are some of the main sources of water. Water from these sources contains substances such as sand, dirt and germs, which make the water impure, and thus, unfit for use.

Water needs to be purified to make it fit for human consumption[1]. Water that is fit for human consumption is called **potable water**.

Things that make the water impure are called **impurities**. Impurities can be soluble or insoluble. **Insoluble impurities** are the ones that do not dissolve in water. **Soluble impurities** are the ones that dissolve in water.

**Word Web**

[1]**Consumption:** eating or drinking

## Removing Insoluble Impurities from Water

Insoluble impurities, such as sand and mud, can be removed by sedimentation and decantation, as well as the filtration methods.

## Activity 5

**Aim:** To understand the processes of sedimentation and decantation

**Materials required:** Two beakers, glass rod, sand and water

**Procedure:**

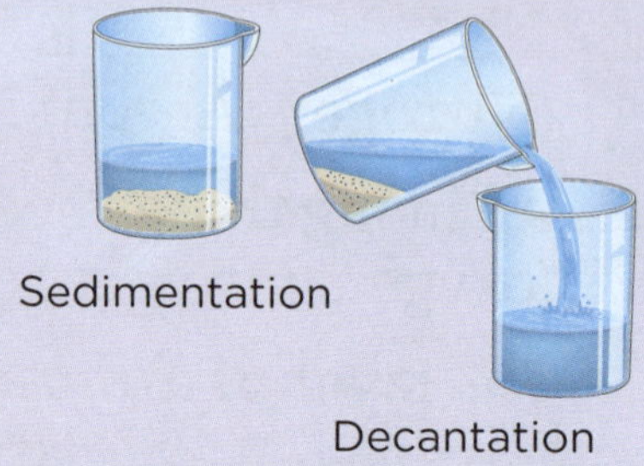


1. Take the beaker containing a mixture of sand and water.
2. Use the glass rod to mix the contents. Leave the beaker undisturbed for some time.
3. The heavier sand particles will settle at the bottom of the beaker, as shown in the figure given alongside. This is called **sedimentation**.
4. Without disturbing the sediment of sand, carefully drain out only the clear water into another beaker as shown in the figure. This is called **decantation**.

The process of the separating solid particles from a liquid medium using a filter paper is known as **filtration**.

## Activity 6

**Aim:** To understand the process of filtration

**Materials required:** Two beakers, glass rod, filter paper, funnel, soil and water

**Procedure:**

1. Take some soil in a beaker and add some water to it. Use a glass rod to mix the contents.
2. Take a filter paper and make a cone, as shown in the given pictures.
3. Place the paper cone in the funnel. Now, place the funnel on the mouth of another beaker.
4. Gently pour the mixture of soil and water over the filter paper.
5. You will notice clear water dripping through the funnel into the beaker, while soil particles get retained in the filter paper.
6. The clear water that gets collected in the beaker after passing through the filter paper is called the filtrate.

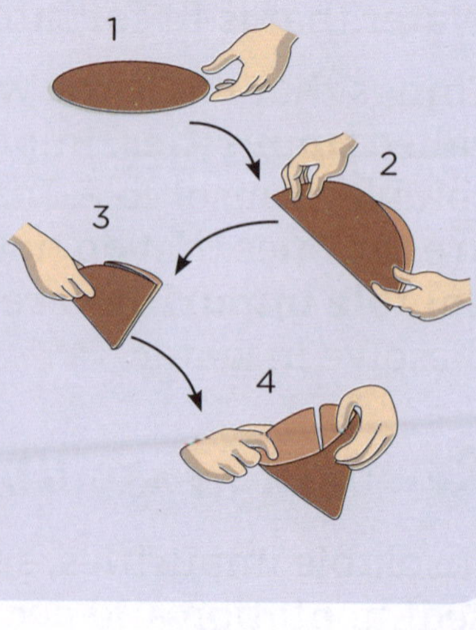

### Applications of filtration in daily life

- Vacuum cleaners have filters to trap dust particles.
- Water taps usually have filters to purify water.
- Coffee makers have filters to keep coffee grounds out of coffee.
- Air conditioners have filter to trap the dust particles present in the air.

Vacuum cleaner

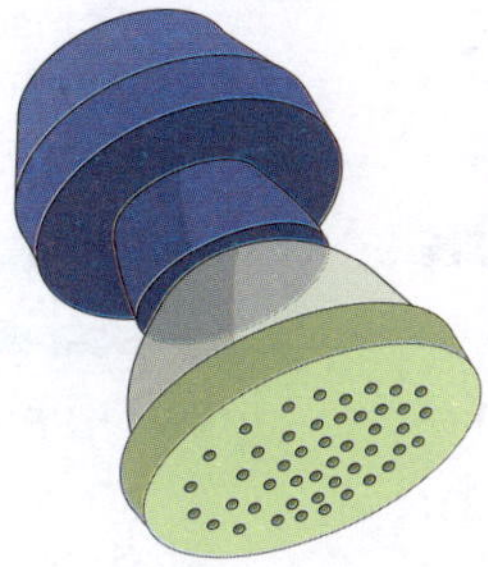
Water tap

Coffee filter

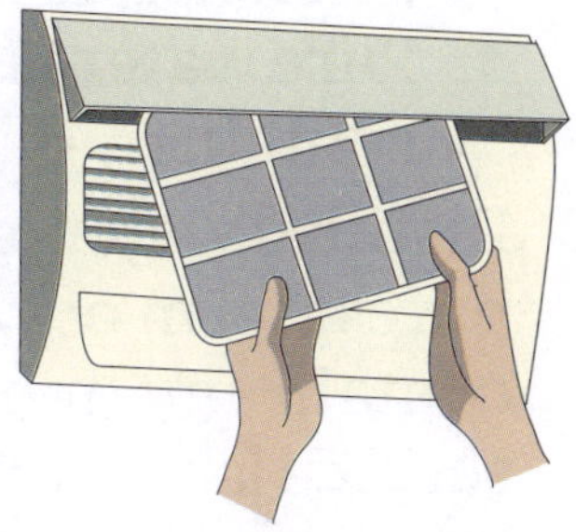
Air conditioner

## Removing Soluble Impurities from Water

The soluble impurities in water can be removed through the evaporation and distillation methods.

Common salt (otherwise called sodium chloride) is extracted from seawater by the process of evaporation under the sun. Let us perform an activity to understand this process.

### Activity 7

**Aim:** To understand the process of obtaining salt from seawater by evaporation

**Materials required:** A shallow dish, saltwater and Bunsen burner

**Procedure:**

1. Set up the apparatus, as shown in the picture.
2. Add saltwater to the shallow dish and heat it till all the water evaporates.

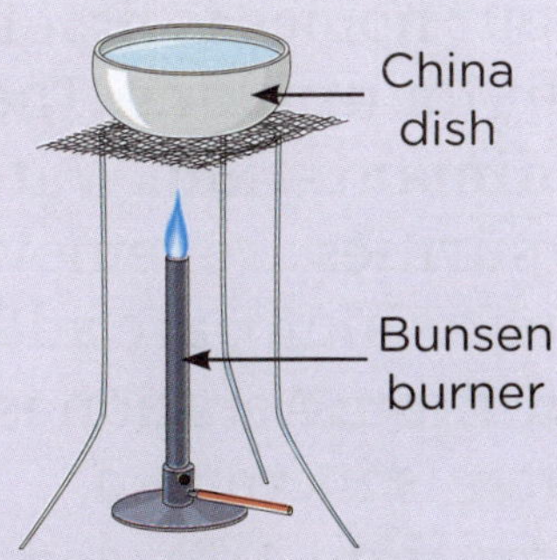


**Observation:** As the water evaporates, we can see salt getting deposited along the inner walls of the dish.

**Distillation** is a process that can be used to separate a pure liquid from a mixture of liquids, due to the difference in their boiling points.

The process involves the following steps:

1. Impure water is heated in a round-bottom flask.
2. Water evaporates to form water vapour and the impurities are left behind.
3. Water vapour passes through the condenser and cools down to form water.
4. Pure water is collected in a separate container.

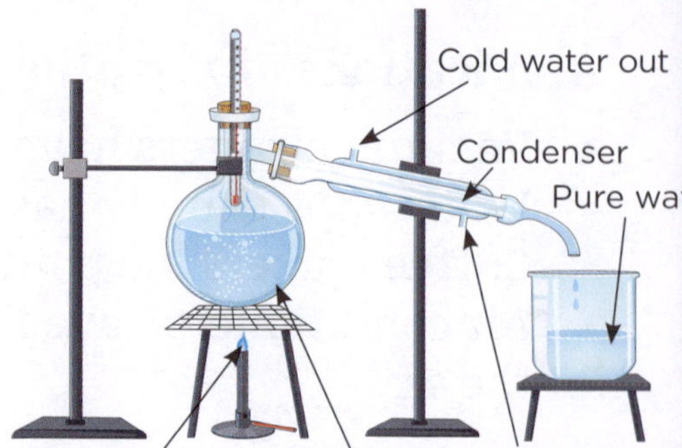

Apparatus for distillation of water

Distilled water is considered to be the purest form of water, as it does not contain any impurities. It is used in science laboratories, car batteries and medicines.

**Science in Context**

Diseases produced by germs in water are called waterborne diseases. Example: typhoid

## PURIFICATION OF DRINKING WATER

a

**Water purification** is the process of removing germs and other harmful substances from water to make it fit for consumption.

At home, we can purify water by boiling it for about 10 minutes. It is the simplest way of purifying water.

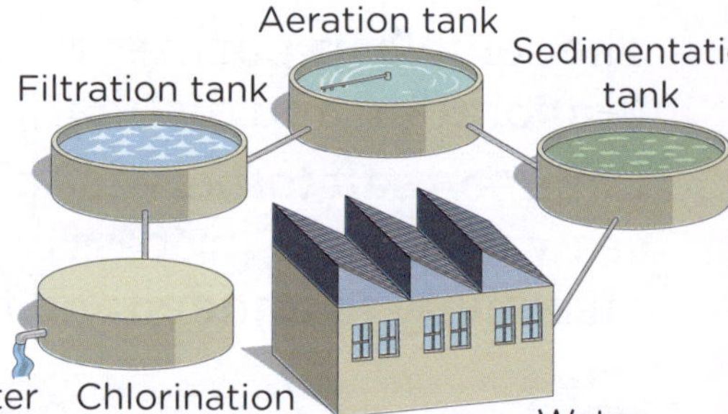

Purification of water

The drinking water that is supplied to our homes is first treated to make it fit for drinking. The following steps are used in the process.

**Sedimentation:** Water is collected in large tanks, where a lot of impurities are removed by the process of sedimentation. Chemicals, such as alum, are added to increase the rate of sedimentation.

**Aeration:** Aeration is a process in which the oxygen content of the water is increased.

**Filtration:** After sedimentation, finer impurities are removed by the process of filtration.

**Chlorination:** It is the process of adding chlorine to water to kill harmful germs found in water. Chlorination can be done at any point during the water purification process.

The purified water is then supplied to our homes.

## Keywords

**Atmosphere:** The thick envelope of air that surrounds the Earth

**Potable water:** Water that is fit for human consumption

**Sedimentation:** The process of the deposition of solid impurities present in a liquid

**Filtration:** The process of separating solid particles from a liquid using a filter paper

**Filtrate:** The clear water that gets collected in the beaker after passing through the filter paper

**Distillation:** The process of separating a pure liquid from a mixture of liquids

**Aeration:** The process of adding oxygen to water during the water purification process

**Chlorination:** The process of adding chlorine to water to kill harmful germs in water

## Summary

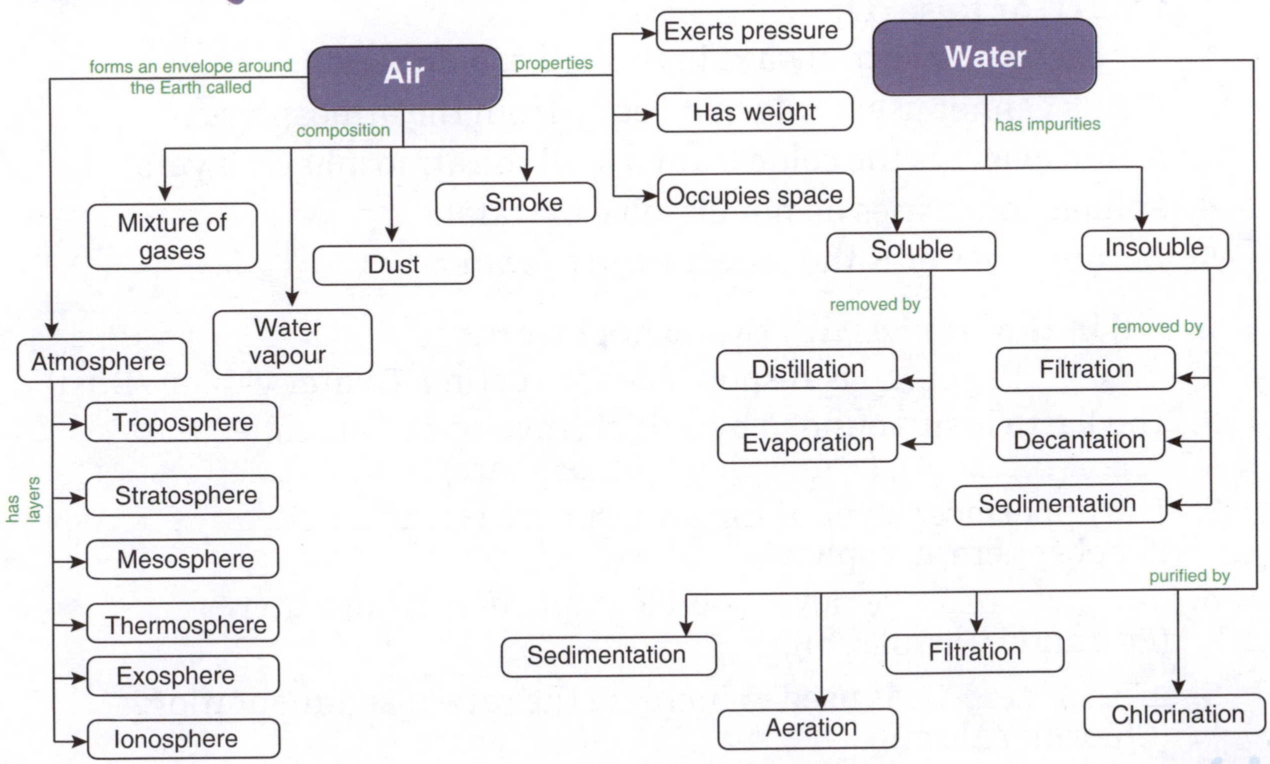

# Exercise

W

**A. Choose the correct option for each of the following.** ia

1. The most abundant gas in the atmosphere is ____________.
   (a) nitrogen (b) oxygen
   (c) carbon dioxide (d) water vapour
2. ________________ is the gas that is used in photosynthesis.
   (a) Oxygen (b) Nitrogen
   (c) Carbon dioxide (d) Argon
3. Where is the ozone layer found?
   (a) Troposphere (b) Stratosphere
   (c) Mesosphere (d) Exosphere
4. In water purification, alum is added during the process of ____________.
   (a) sedimentation (b) filtration (c) aeration (d) chlorination
5. Which of the following chemicals is used to kill germs during water purification?
   (a) Fertilizer (b) Alum (c) Chlorine (d) Argon

**B. State whether the following statements are true (T) or false (F).** ia

1. Air exerts pressure always in the upward direction.
2. Plants cannot use nitrogen directly from the atmosphere.
3. Stratosphere is the coldest among all the atmospheric layers.
4. Soluble impurities do not dissolve in water.
5. Decanted water is the purest form of water.

**C. Fill in the blanks with the correct words.** ia

1. ________________ is responsible for rusting. (Water vapour/Dust)
2. The Earth is surrounded by a thick envelope of air called the ________________. (atmosphere/ionosphere)
3. The uppermost layer of the atmosphere is ____________. (troposphere/exosphere)
4. ________________ removes soluble impurities from water. (Filtration/Distillation)
5. ________________ is used to increase the rate of sedimentation. (Chlorine/Alum)

**D. Give two examples for each of the following.**

1. Properties of air
2. Gases present in the air
3. Applications of air pressure
4. Processes of removing insoluble impurities from water
5. Uses of distilled water

**E. Give reasons for the following.**

1. An inflated balloon is heavier than the one which is not.
2. An astronaut needs an oxygen cylinder when he travels to the space.
3. Filter papers can be used to separate solids from liquids.
4. Air conditioners have removable filters in them.
5. Distilled water is the purest form of water.

**F. Answer the following questions briefly.**

1. What is air pressure?
2. Name the different layers of the atmosphere.
3. How does the ozone layer protect the Earth?
4. Why should we drink purified water?
5. Write any two applications of filtration in daily life.

**G. Answer the following questions.**

1. What is the difference between troposphere and stratosphere? Explain.
2. How will you prove that air exerts pressure? Explain with the help of a diagram.
3. Define distillation, and list the steps involved in this process.
4. Explain the steps involved in water purification before its supply to our homes.

## Cognitive Corner

### Critical Thinking

1. You have to separate orange juice from its pulp. Which out of these processes would you use: sedimentation and decantation, or filtration? Why?
2. Iron grills in our windows and gates are painted.
3. Astronauts cannot survive without oxygen cylinders in space. Why?

## Picture Study

Label the parts of the distillation apparatus given below.

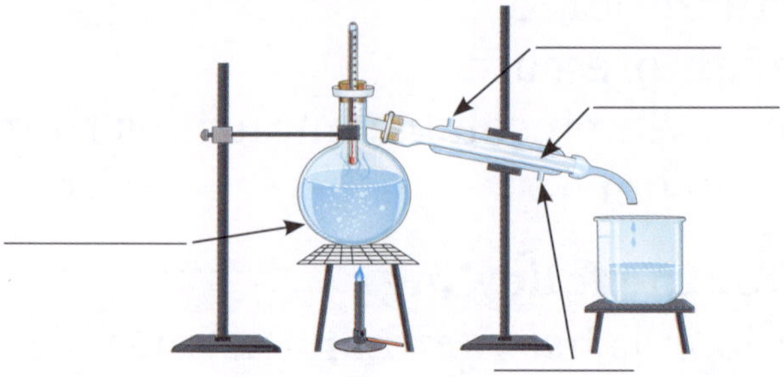

## Project

1. On a chart paper, draw the process of water purification. Explain each step.
2. Nowadays, a lot of water purifiers are available in the market. With the help of an elder, find out how they work, collect pictures and prepare a report.

## Life Skills

Water is a precious resource and every drop of it should be saved. Some of the ways to save water are shown below.

**Turn off taps** while brushing your teeth, soaping clothes and scrubbing vessels.

**Fixing leaking taps** does not take much, but it can save a significant amount of water.

**Using a bucket** instead of a shower to bathe can reduce your water consumption by 80 per cent!

Energy-star-rated dishwashers and washing machines use less water.

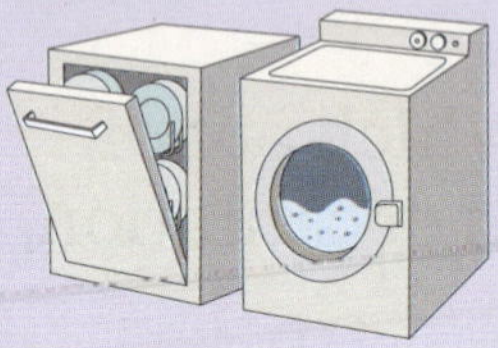

Low-flow showerheads and toilets with smaller flush tanks use less water.

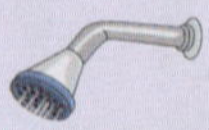

To recycle water on your own, do simple things, such as using the water in which vegetables have been washed to water plants.

Suggest some more ways by which you can save water at home.

# Worksheet

The atmosphere exerts a lot of pressure on the surface of the Earth. How do we not feel the pressure exerted by the air? There is just as much pressure inside our body pressing outward as there is air pressure pressing down on us. They typically cancel out. That is why, we do not feel the pressure exerted by the air on us.

Air pressure is greater closer to the Earth and decreases as we go up into space. That is why, astronauts need special spacesuits to travel into space.

Do a research and find out what makes a spacesuit special. Also, find out how it protects the body of an astronaut.

Astronauts in space

___________________________________________

___________________________________________

___________________________________________

___________________________________________

___________________________________________

___________________________________________

# 7 Earth, Sun and Moon

### Learning Checklist

- The solar system
- Sun
- Earth
- Moon
- Eclipses

## Let's Get Started

Identify the objects shown in the pictures below that we normally see in the sky.

______________

______________

______________

Objects seen in the sky are called **celestial objects**. The sun and the other celestial objects that revolve around it form the solar system.

Let us learn more about the solar system, the sun, the Earth and the moon.

## THE SOLAR SYSTEM

a

The sun and the eight planets that revolve around it together form the **solar system**. Other than the planets, satellites[1] of various planets, comets and asteroids are also part of the solar system.

> **Word Web**
>
> [1]**Satellite:** a celestial object that moves around a planet

The sun is at the centre of the solar system. There are **eight** planets revolving around the sun. These planets are Mercury, Venus, Earth, Mars, Jupiter, Saturn, Uranus and Neptune. They revolve around the sun in fixed paths called **orbits**.

Mercury is the smallest planet and is also the closest planet to the sun. Venus is the hottest and brightest planet. The Earth is also called the blue planet. It is the only planet where life is known to exist. Mars is also called the red planet. Jupiter is the largest planet of the solar system. Saturn is the second largest planet after Jupiter. It has rings around it. Saturn is so light that if there was a tub of water big enough to hold it, it would float in it. Uranus is the coldest planet of the solar system. Neptune is the planet farthest from the sun.

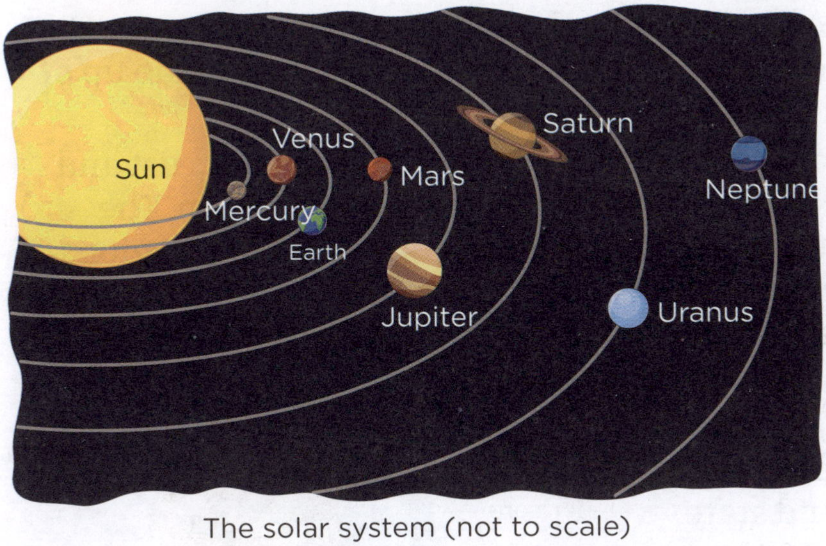


The solar system (not to scale)

> **Science in Context**
>
> Pluto, which was earlier considered as the ninth planet, is now known as a 'dwarf' planet.

## SUN

The sun is a star that is situated at the centre of our solar system. It is a huge ball of burning gases. Its size is about 109 times that of the Earth.

Its mass is about 330,000 times that of the Earth. It is almost 99.86% of the total mass of the solar system.

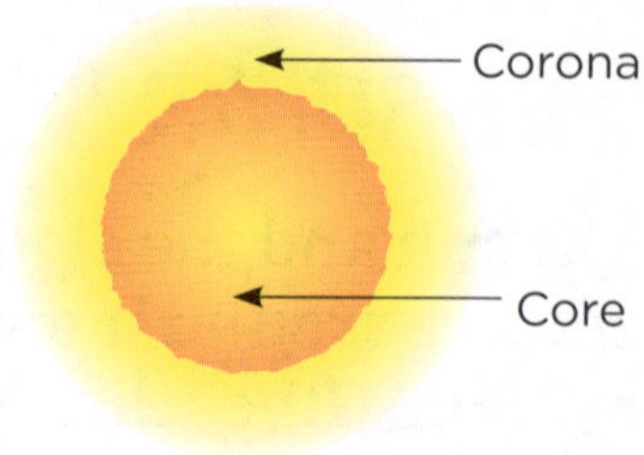


Hydrogen and helium gases are the major constituents of the sun. The sun has a thin outer layer called the **corona** and a central part called the **core**.

In the core of the sun, hydrogen gas continuously gets converted into helium.  A very large amount of heat and light energy is released during this process. Energy released by the sun is called **solar energy**. The temperature on its surface is about 6000°C. All living things on the Earth ultimately depend on solar energy for their existence.

## EARTH

The Earth is the third planet from the sun. It is surrounded by an envelope of air known as the **atmosphere**. The atmosphere of the Earth protects us from the harmful radiations of the sun. The interior part of the Earth is divided into three main layers: crust, mantle and core.

**Crust** is the outermost layer of the Earth. Its thickness ranges from about 5 km below the ocean floor to about 70 km below the land. The continents and the oceans are present on this layer. It is made up of rocks and contains all the things essential for life.

**Mantle** is the middle layer of the Earth, lying between the crust and the core. The thickness of the mantle extends up to 2,890 km. The outer region of the mantle consists of solid rocks. The inner regions of the mantle consist of molten rocks. During volcanic eruptions, magma comes out from this layer to the surface of the Earth.

**Core** is the innermost layer of the Earth. It is mainly composed of iron and nickel. The outer core is in a molten liquid state. It extends to about 3,400 km. The inner core is a solid sphere of mostly iron situated about 1,220 km from the outer core.

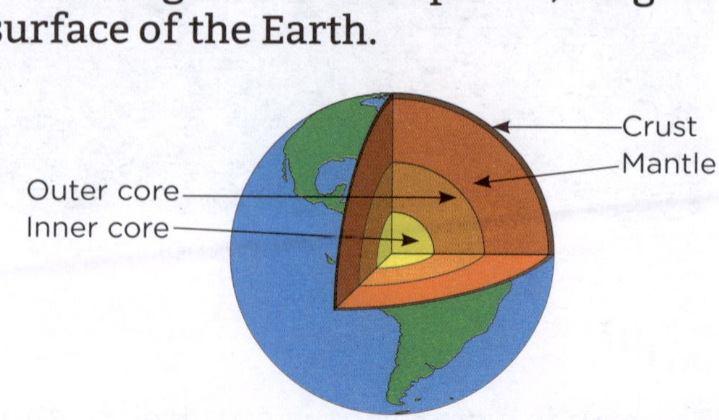


Internal structure of the Earth

## Revise and Recall

**Fill in the blanks with the correct words.**

1. The outer thin layer of the sun is called the ____________. (core/corona)
2. In the core of the sun, ____________ gets converted into helium. (hydrogen/nitrogen)
3. The interior part of the Earth is divided into ____________ main layers. (three/five)
4. The middle layer of the Earth is called the ____________. (mantle/crust)
5. The major element in the inner core is ____________. (iron/gold)

# MOON

An object that revolves around a planet is called a **satellite**. Satellites are of two types: natural satellites and artificial satellites. Naturally existing objects revolving around a planet are called **natural satellites**. Some satellites of the Earth are man-made satellites. They are called **artificial satellites**.

Surface of the moon

The moon is the natural satellite of the Earth. It revolves around the Earth in an orbit at a distance of about 384,400 km from the Earth. The moon has no light of its own. It shines in the sky, because it reflects the sunlight falling on its surface. It is almost spherical in shape. It has no atmosphere, due to which it is very hot during the day and very cold at night.

The surface of the moon has a lot of craters. These are formed when huge rocks called meteorites[1] hit its surface. There are also lots of mountains on its surface.

**Word Web**

[1]**Meteorites:** rocks from outer space

**Landing on the moon:** Neil Armstrong was the first man to step on the moon followed minutes later by Edwin Aldrin on 20th July 1969. They were the astronauts along with Michael Collins in the American space mission, Apollo 11.

Astronaut on the moon

The rocks that they brought from the surface of the moon helped the scientists to obtain a lot of information about the moon.

There were some unmanned missions to the moon which obtained a lot of information about its surface through photographs.

**Chandrayaan Mission**

Chandrayaan-1 was India's first unmanned mission to the moon. It was launched on 22 October 2008 from Satish Dhawan Space Centre, Sriharikota, Andhra Pradesh. The mission helped to obtain a lot of information about the moon.

## Phases of the Moon

When we look at the moon, it appears to change its shape every night. Sometimes it is a round ball, sometimes C-shaped and sometimes it disappears completely. This happens because we see only that part of the moon that reflects the sun's light as it moves around the Earth in its orbit. These varied shapes of the moon are called the **phases of the moon.**

# ECLIPSES

a

An **eclipse** is a natural phenomenon in which one celestial object (or a portion of it) becomes temporarily invisible as it is hidden by the shadow of another celestial object. It happens when three celestial objects are in a straight line.

The revolution of the Earth around the sun and the revolution of the moon around the Earth cause lunar and solar eclipses.

## Lunar Eclipse

When the Earth comes between the sun and the moon, the shadow of the Earth falls on the moon. This causes a lunar eclipse.

Lunar eclipse can be **partial**, in which a part of the moon may be visible, or **total**, in which the moon is not visible at all. The type and duration of a lunar eclipse depends on the position of the moon in the orbit.

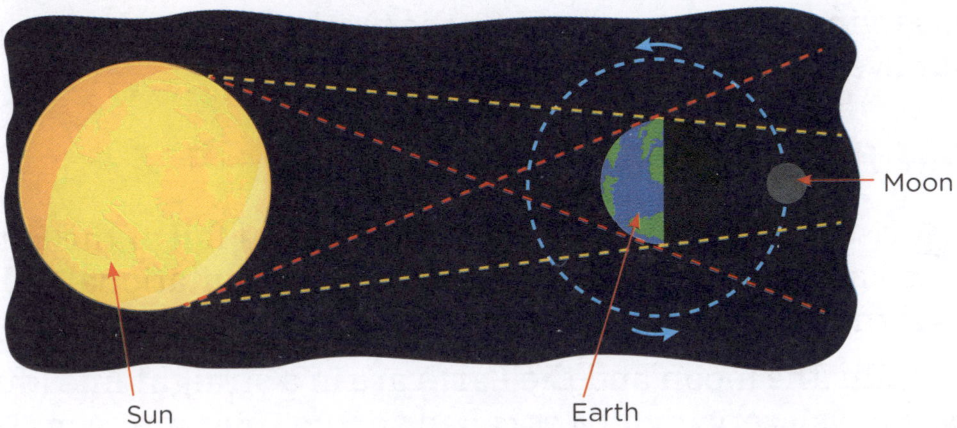

Lunar eclipse

## Solar Eclipse

Solar eclipse occurs when the moon comes between the sun and the Earth, and the shadow of the moon falls on the Earth.

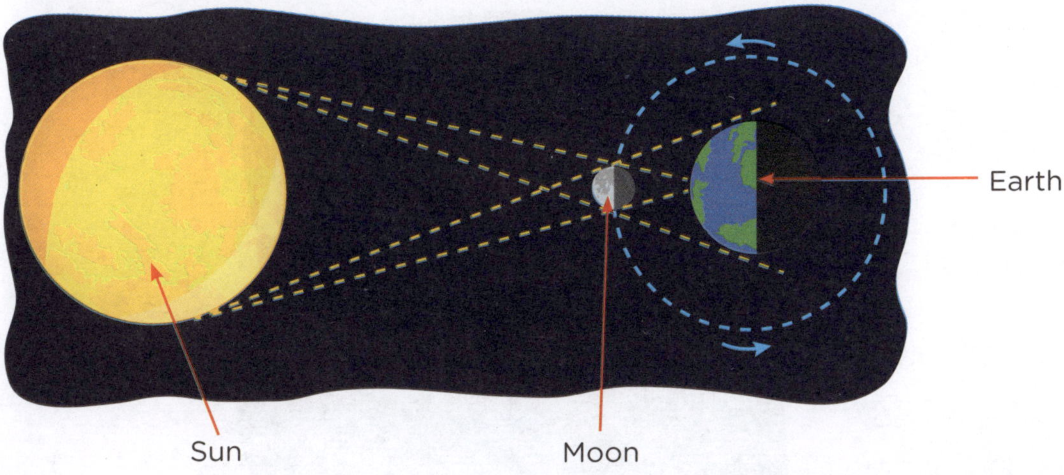

Solar eclipse

If we observe from an area on the Earth where the dark inner shadow of the moon falls, we can see a **total solar eclipse**. If we observe from an area on the Earth where the faint outer shadow of the moon falls, we can see a **partial solar eclipse**. If only a bright ring is seen around a central eclipsed area, then we see a ring-shaped eclipse or **annular eclipse**.

Solar eclipse enables us to study the outer layer of the sun called the corona, which is otherwise very difficult to observe due to its bright rays.

We must always remember to wear UV rays-protected dark glasses while observing the solar eclipse, as the bright light of the sun might harm our eyes.

## Effect of the eclipse on the Earth

Sea water rises and falls twice a day. The rise and fall of the Earth's water (such as water in the oceans) due to the gravitational pull of the moon, and to some extent of the sun, is called a **tide**.

When the sun, the moon and the Earth are in a straight line (during new moon days), very high tides called **spring tides** are seen. The combined force of gravity of the sun and the moon bring about these high tides.

When the sun and the moon are at a right angle to each other, we get very low tides called **neap tides**. They usually occur twice a month during the first and the third quarter of the moon.

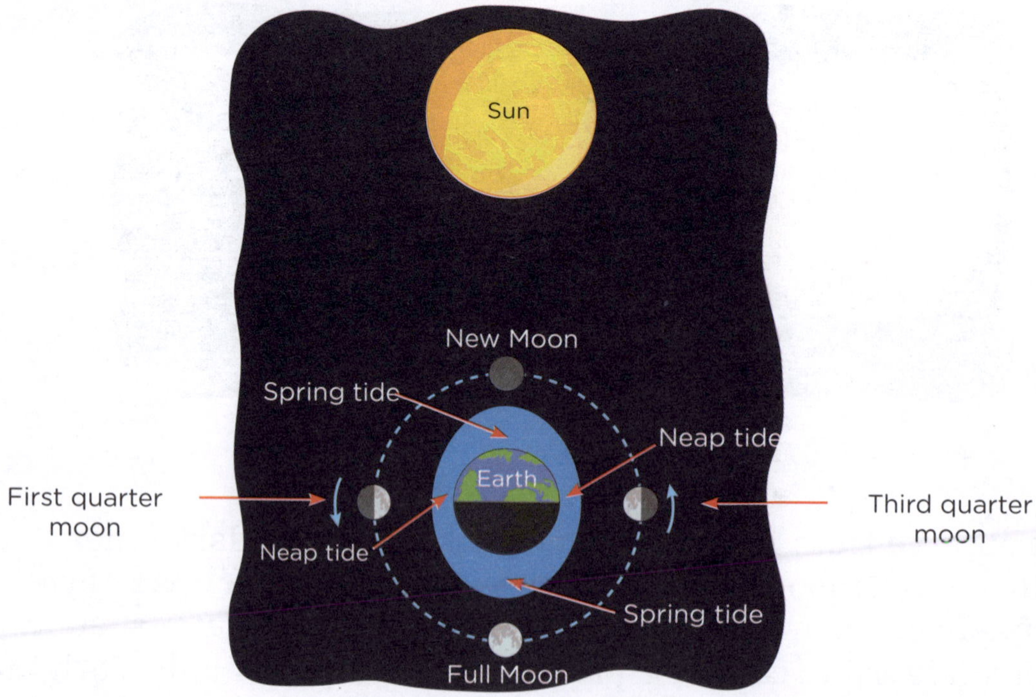


Spring and neap tides

## Keywords

**Crust:** The outermost layer of the Earth

**Mantle:** The middle layer of the Earth, lying between the crust and the core

**Core:** The innermost layer of the Earth

**Satellite:** An object that revolves around a planet

**Lunar eclipse:** The phenomenon in which the moon is covered by the shadow of the Earth

**Solar eclipse:** The phenomenon that occurs when the moon comes between the sun and the Earth and the shadow of the moon falls on the Earth

**Tides:** The rise and fall of the Earth's water due to the gravitational pull of the moon and the sun

## Summary

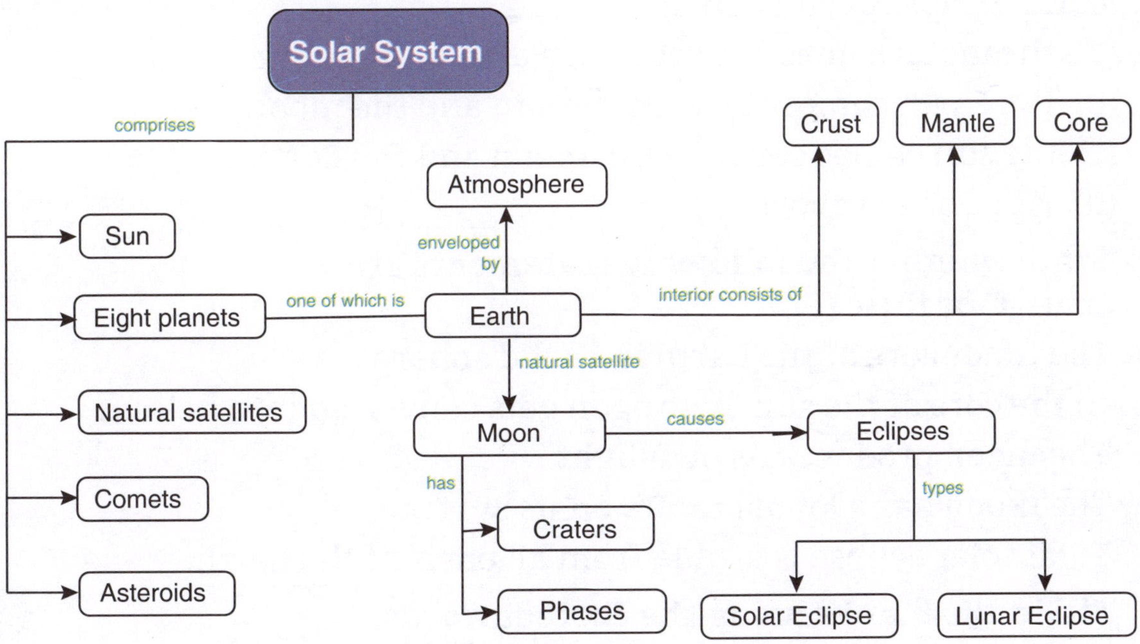

# Exercise

W

**A. Choose the correct option for each of the following.** ia

1. The coldest planet of the solar system is __________ .
   (a) Neptune (b) Uranus (c) Mars (d) Earth
2. Major constituents of the sun are __________ .
   (a) hydrogen and helium
   (b) neon and oxygen
   (c) helium and oxygen
   (d) hydrogen and oxygen
3. Solid rocks are found in the outer region of the __________ .
   (a) core (b) cornea (c) crater (d) mantle
4. Solar eclipse occurs when __________ .
   (a) the moon comes between the Earth and the sun
   (b) the Earth comes between the sun and the moon
   (c) the sun comes between the moon and the Earth
   (d) None of the above
5. Lunar eclipse occurs when __________ .
   (a) the moon comes between the Earth and the sun
   (b) the Earth comes between the sun and the moon
   (c) the sun comes between the moon and the Earth
   (d) None of the above

**B. State whether the following statements are true (T) or false (F).** ia

1. The inner core of the Earth is a solid sphere.
2. In the core of the sun, hydrogen gets converted into helium.
3. The moon produces its own light.
4. The moon has a lot of craters on its surface.
5. Total solar eclipse is visible from all parts of the Earth.

**C. Fill in the blanks using the correct words.** ia

1. The outermost layer of the Earth is called the __________ . (crust/core)
2. During volcanic eruptions, magma comes out from the __________ of the Earth. (crust/mantle)

3. The moon is the ___________ satellite of the Earth. (natural/artificial)
4. The ___________ has no atmosphere. (Earth/moon)
5. Spring tides are seen on ___________ days. (full moon/new moon)

**D. Answer the following in one word.**

1. The fixed path on which planets revolve around the sun
2. The temperature on the surface of the sun
3. Layer of the Earth on which the oceans lie
4. An element present in the core of the Earth
5. Name for the ring-shaped eclipse

**E. Give reasons for the following.**

1. Solar eclipses are important for scientists.
2. Neap tides are low tides.
3. We can see only phases of the moon from the Earth.
4. Moon only reflects sun's light.
5. The sun is our ultimate source of energy.

**F. Answer the following questions briefly.**

1. What is the solar system?
2. What are artificial satellites?
3. What is an eclipse? Name the two eclipses that are visible to us.
4. What is the difference between a total solar eclipse and a partial solar eclipse?
5. What is an annular eclipse?
6. What are tides? How are they formed?

**G. Answer the following questions.**

1. Write a note on the features of the sun.
2. Explain the different layers of the Earth.
3. Explain the features of the surface of the moon.
4. How does a lunar eclipse occur?
5. How does a solar eclipse occur?

# Cognitive Corner

## Critical Thinking

1. There was an article in a newspaper regarding an eclipse with the title "Viewing an eclipse is dangerous''. Which eclipse is this article related to? Can you suggest ways to view the eclipse safely?
2. A lunar eclipse occurs only on a full moon day. Why?
3. One of your classmates is of the opinion that solar and lunar eclipses occur because the Earth and the moon are opaque. Do you agree with this? Why or why not ?

## Picture Study

Label the different layers in the internal structure of the Earth.

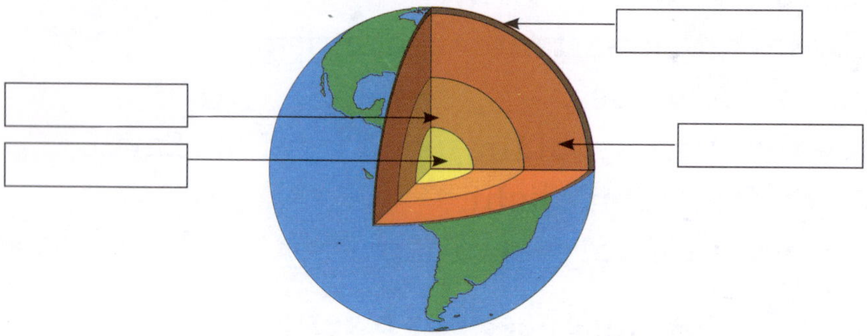

## Project

Using a torch, a big ball, a small ball and a screen, we can demonstrate lunar eclipse. Place the torch and the screen on a table. Light the torch and place a big ball between the torch and the screen.

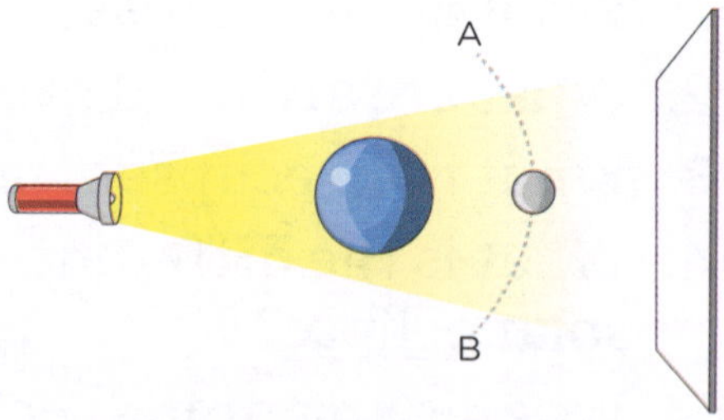


Now, place the small ball at point A, as shown in the diagram. You can see the shadows of both the balls on the screen. Move the small ball along the line, from A to B. You cannot see the shadow of the small ball when it enters in the shadow of the big ball, and again, as you move the ball further, the shadow appears.

## Life Skills

Suppose the astronauts who land on the moon decide to stay there forever. Would they be able to survive there? Give reasons for your answer.

# Worksheet

Asteroid belt

The solar system comprises the sun and its family of eight planets, their satellites, comets and asteroids. Asteroids are pieces of rocks of all shapes and sizes which revolve around the sun. Most of the asteroids are found in the space between Mars and Jupiter.

An asteroid impact on the Earth destroyed the dinosaurs and made the Earth inhabitable for a number of centuries.

There is always a chance of another asteroid hitting the Earth. So, scientists and astronomers keep a lookout for them. They are thinking of ways to deflect the asteroid if any happen to come towards the Earth.

A space probe called Hayabusa2 was launched by the Japanese apace agency on 3 December 2014. The probe landed on a nearby asteroid on 27 June 2018. It stayed there for a year and a half and took samples of the material of which the asteroid is made. It left the asteroid in November 2019 with the samples and landed on the Earth on 6 December 2020.

Draw and colour a scene of an asteroid approaching the Earth. Suggest any one method of how the asteroid can be prevented from reaching the Earth.

# 8 Our Environment

## Learning Checklist

- Pollution of air, water, land and noise
- Saving the environment

## Let's Get Started

Human beings have made their environment dirty in many ways. Look at the pictures given below and tick the ones that make the environment dirty.

## ENVIRONMENT

The things around us form our environment.

Our environment contains both living things and non-living things. All living, including us, depend on non-living things. For example, we need air to breathe and water to drink. We get these from the environment around us.

A natural environment

The food we eat also comes from plants and animals. We get raw materials, such as soil, sand, stones, etc., from the Earth to build our homes and buildings.

## POLLUTION

a

The addition of harmful substances to the environment, which makes it dirty, is called **pollution**.

The substances that cause pollution are called **pollutants**. Pollution has harmful effects on plants, animals and human beings.

## AIR POLLUTION

The air in the cities contains a lot of impurities. Smoke from industries and vehicles is the main source of air pollution. In the villages, many houses still use firewood and coal for cooking. This gives out smoke, causing air pollution in the rural areas. Smoke from firecrackers also contributes to air pollution. People who breathe in the polluted air suffer from respiratory diseases, such as asthma, breathing problems and lung cancer.

Bursting of firecrackers causes air pollution

Burning of wood causes air pollution

Smoke from factories and vehicles causes air pollution

Gases such as carbon dioxide and methane trap the heat from the sun and do not allow it to escape from the Earth's atmosphere. This is called the **greenhouse effect**. Over the years, the increase in the amount of carbon dioxide in the atmosphere due to air pollution has led to a gradual rise in the Earth's temperature. This is called **global warming**. Global warming can cause the ice at the polar regions to melt, leading to a rise in the water level of the oceans, which results in floods.

## WATER POLLUTION

a

The main sources of water pollution are the wastes from industries, and the sewage pipelines that come from homes and other buildings. In the villages, the lakes or rivers are polluted due to the various activities done in or near the water source. Villagers depend on the lake or river for washing clothes and bathing cattle. The dirt and soap from all this washing goes into the water and causes pollution. The solid wastes dumped in the water also causes water pollution.

Sewage let into the water source

Seas and oceans have a threat from oil spillage from ships that transport oil. This oil does not mix with the water, and harms the lives of the plants and animals living in these water bodies.

Various causes of water pollution

Pollution of water makes it unfit for human use. Sewage contains harmful germs that cause diseases such as cholera, diarrhoea and typhoid. If these germs are present in drinking water, they can cause diseases.

## Science in Context

The Exxon-Valdez oil spill in Alaska happened on March 24, 1989. A tanker was carrying 55 million US gallons of crude oil. It met with an accident, causing the spillage of the oil into the seawater. This caused the loss of life of many animals such as sea otters, seals, bald eagles and seabirds. Fish population in the sea was disturbed, and the decrease in fish population caused a huge loss to the people working in the fishing industry.

# LAND POLLUTION

Dumping wastes, such as plastic bags, glass and metal, containers causes land pollution. Overuse of chemicals such as fertilizers, insecticides and pesticides also causes land pollution.

Soil is held together by the roots of trees. Deforestation or cutting of trees makes the soil loose. This loose soil is easily carried away by the blowing wind. The rainwater also washes away the loose soil. The process of the removal of the top layer of soil by wind and rainwater is called **soil erosion**.

Garbage dumped in the soil causing land pollution

Soil erosion

## Revise and Recall

**Fill in the blanks with the correct words.**

1. Smoke from automobiles causes ___________ pollution. (land/air)
2. The wastes from industries and the sewage pipelines are the sources of ________________ pollution. (water/air)
3. Dumping wastes, such as plastic bags, glass and metal containers, causes ________________ pollution. (air/land)
4. The roots of trees hold the ________________ together. (soil/water)

## NOISE POLLUTION

Noise pollution in a city

Noise pollution is caused by loud sounds that disturb the normal activities of human beings and animals.

Honking of vehicles, sound from the loud speakers, television, etc., cause noise pollution.

Noise from firecrackers, the construction of buildings, and roads also cause noise pollution.

Noise pollution has many adverse health effects, such as hypertension, hearing impairment, increase in the risk of heart disease, and sleep disturbance.

## SAVING THE ENVIRONMENT

We should try to minimize pollution to save our environment. Some of the ways of reducing pollution are given below:

- Reducing air pollution by using vehicles only when needed, and walking or cycling to short distances.
- The smoke and gases produced from the factories should be processed and made safe before they are let out through chimneys.
- Planting more trees to reduce air pollution, get pure air to breathe and to prevent soil erosion.
- Treatment of the waste obtained from the factories and the sewage from homes before being let into water bodies.
- Proper management and the disposal of garbage.
- Using environment-friendly manures and natural fertilizers in fields.
- Using cloth bags instead of polythene bags and minimizing the use of plastics.
- Construction of factories far away from the main city.
- Use of solar energy should be encouraged, as it does not cause pollution.

## Keywords

**Pollution:** The addition of harmful substances to the environment, which makes it dirty

**Pollutants:** The substances that cause pollution

**Greenhouse effect:** The trapping of heat by the gases in the atmosphere that leads to an increase in the Earth's temperature

**Global warming:** A gradual rise in the Earth's temperature due to the greenhouse effect

## Summary

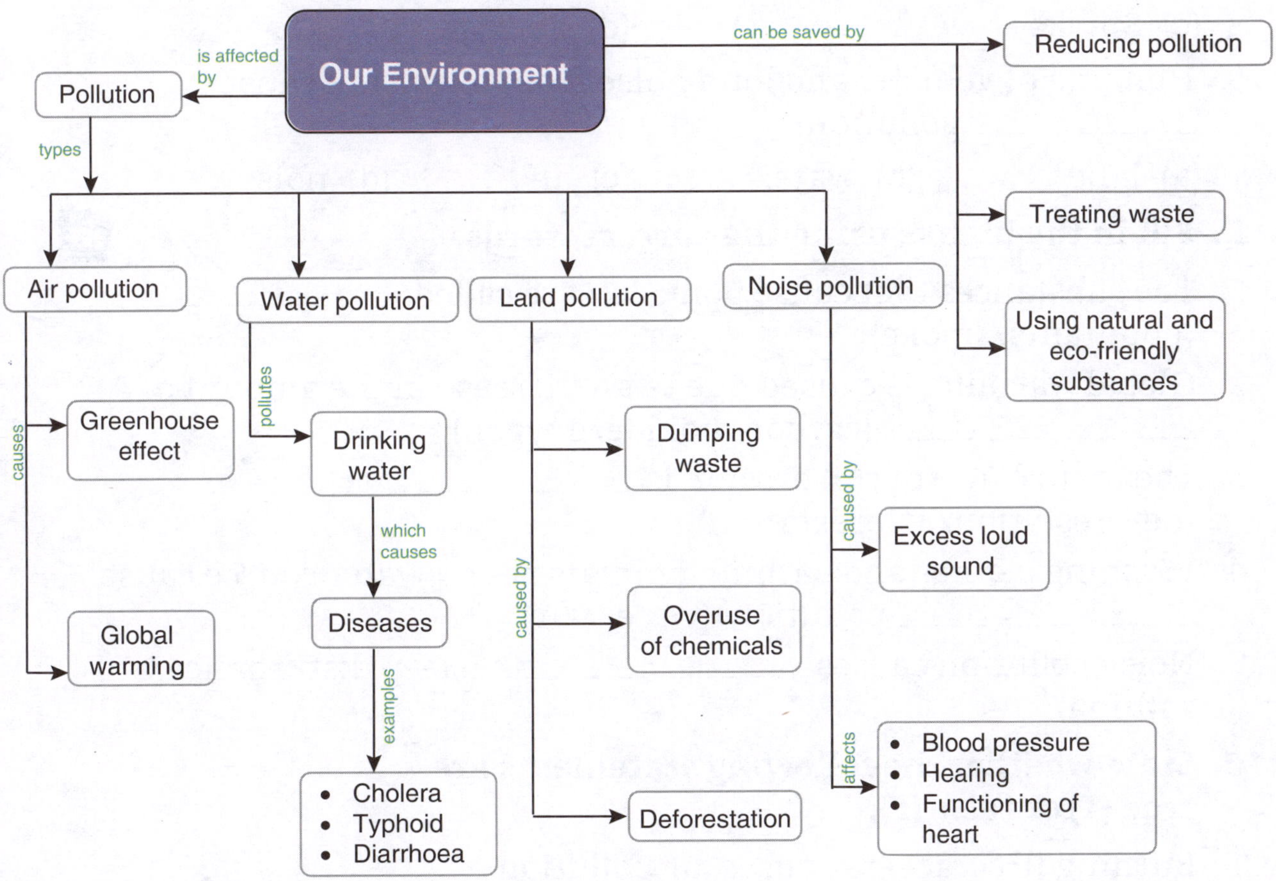

# Exercise

**A. Choose the correct option for each of the following.**

1. Which of the following is a cause of air pollution?
   (a) Trees (b) Smoke (c) House (d) All of these
2. Which of the following is not a cause of soil erosion?
   (a) Wind (b) Rain (d) Trees (d) None of these
3. Air pollution can cause ______________.
   (a) asthma (b) obesity
   (c) hearing impairment (d) cholera
4. Which of these causes land pollution?
   (a) Loudspeakers (b) Polythene bags
   (c) Smoke (d) Sewage
5. Honking of vehicles and loud noise from television cause ______________ pollution.
   (a) land (b) water (c) air (d) noise

**B. Fill in the blanks using the correct words.**

1. The substances that cause pollution are called ______________. (pollutants/smoke)
2. Global warming is caused due to an increase in the amount of ______________. (carbon dioxide/oxygen)
3. The main cause of soil erosion is ______________. (deforestation/afforestation)
4. Washing clothes and bathing animals near a water source cause ______________ pollution. (water/air)
5. Noise pollution causes ______________. (sleep disturbance/asthma)

**C. State whether the following statements are true (T) or false (F).**

1. Burning firecrackers causes air pollution.
2. Global warming can cause the melting of ice in the Polar regions.
3. Oil spillage from ships causes water pollution.
4. Sewage contains germs that cause cholera, diarrhoea, etc.
5. Pollution of air, water, noise and land is beneficial for us.

**D. Give two examples for each of the following.**

1. Kinds of pollution
2. Activities that cause water pollution
3. Causes of soil erosion
4. Wastes that cause land pollution
5. Health effects of noise pollution

**E. Give reasons for the following.**

1. Planting more trees reduces soil erosion as well as controls the greenhouse effect.
2. Reducing the levels of methane and carbon dioxide in the atmosphere is essential for our survival.
3. Treating sewage water is good for the environment.
4. We must reduce the use of chemicals such as fertilizers and insecticides.
5. Drinking untreated water causes diseases.

**F. Answer the following questions briefly.**

1. What is pollution?
2. What are pollutants?
3. Write the harmful effects of air pollution.
4. What is global warming?
5. What is soil erosion?

**G. Answer the following questions.**

1. Write a note on air pollution.
2. What are the causes of water pollution in cities and villages?
3. What is land pollution? Mention two human activities that cause land pollution.
4. Describe the sources of noise pollution.
5. Write any five ways to save our environment.

# Cognitive Corner

## Critical Thinking

1. What does the sign given alongside signify? Where is this sign usually found?
2. Bursting firecrackers can be replaced with many other activities that save the environment. Justify the statement.
3. What are water pollutants? Write any one water pollutant and devise a plan to remove that pollutant.
4. In India, Delhi has huge machines which pump fresh air into the atmosphere. Why does the urban administration take such measures?

## Picture Study

Tick the things that can be used to reduce pollution.

 ☐

 ☐

 ☐

 ☐

 ☐

## Project

Make posters about the four types of pollution you have studied in this chapter and the ways to prevent them. Write catchy slogans to create awareness.

## Life Skills

Reusing some of the waste generated at home can prevent land pollution. Growing plants in waste materials collected at home, such as empty cans, bottles, old shoes, tires, etc., is one such way.

Collect old ceramic mugs or plastic bottles from your house. With the help of your parents, grow plants or herbs, such as coriander, in them. You can also decorate them to look attractive. Gift these planters to your friends or relatives.

# Worksheet

We are all aware how air, water, soil and noise pollution are destroying the Earth and causing climate change. We know the main causes of such pollution. How can we, in our small way, help in reducing the pollution?

A. Identify the type of pollution depicted in the images given below and mention two causes of each.

---

---

One of the major causes of both types of pollution depicted above is vehicles. If we ride bicycles, we can reduce both air and sound pollution.

There is one more advantage to cycling. It is a great form of exercise and will keep us fit and energetic.

B. Write any two habits other than cycling which reduce pollution (of any type) and keep us healthy.

---

---

# 9 Natural Disasters

## Learning Checklist

- Earthquake
- Volcanoes
- Tidal waves and tsunami
- Floods
- Drought

## Let's Get Started

Look at the pictures shown below. Can you identify the given phenomena? Choose the words from the help box.

| Earthquake | Drought | Thunderstorm | Volcanic eruption |
|---|---|---|---|

____________________

____________________

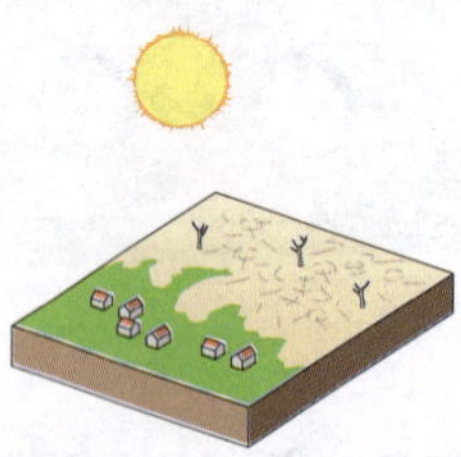

____________________

____________________

A **disaster** is defined as an unexpected event resulting in great damage, loss and destruction to life and property. Natural events occurring on the Earth, that cause great damage and/or loss of life, are called **natural disasters**.

In this chapter, we will learn more about natural disasters.

# EARTHQUAKE

The sudden movement of a part of the Earth's surface is called an **earthquake**. These movements are caused by the shifting of the layers of rocks deep under the Earth's crust. The actual point deep inside the Earth, where an earthquake begins, is called the **focus**, and the point on the Earth's surface directly above the focus is called the **epicentre**. The maximum effect of the earthquake is felt at the epicentre and the effect reduces as we move away from it.

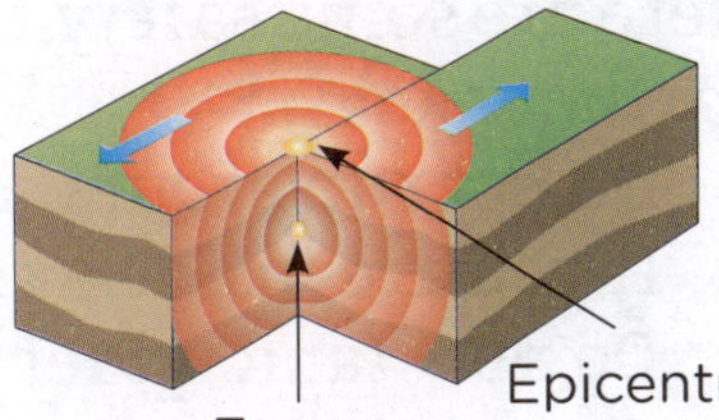


## After-effects of Earthquakes

- Destruction of buildings, trees, roads and vehicles
- Huge loss of life (humans and animals)
- Spread of diseases

Destruction caused by an earthquake

## Measuring Earthquakes and Their Effects

The effects of earthquakes depend on the force with which they occur. Some earthquakes are so weak that they just shake materials kept on a shelf, while some are so strong that they cause buildings to fall down and lead to the deaths of numerous people.

**Word Web**

[1]**Magnitude:** relative size or extent

The intensity and duration of an earthquake can be measured by using an instrument called the **seismograph**. **Richter scale** is a standard scale used to find out the magnitude[1] of earthquakes on a scale of 1 to 10. Earthquakes measuring 1 to 2 on the scale will hardly be felt. Earthquakes measuring 3, 4 and 5 on the scale can cause damage to property. Earthquakes measuring 6 and above on the scale can result in widespread damage to property and also cause death.

**Wonder!**

Zhang Heng of China's Han dynasty was the first person to build an instrument that could detect earthquakes.

Modern seismograph

## Safety Measures During an Earthquake

Here are some safety measures you can take to be safe during an earthquake:

- Do not run around in panic.
- If you are inside a room, take shelter under a table or a bed.
- Do not stand under or near objects that can fall and hurt you.
- Do not use an elevator if you are on the upper floors. Always use the staircase.
- If you are outdoors, stand in an open area away from any buildings and trees.

## VOLCANOES

a

The core of the Earth is made up of molten rock called **magma**. A crack or vent on the Earth's surface that allows hot magma from below the surface to come out is called a **volcano**.

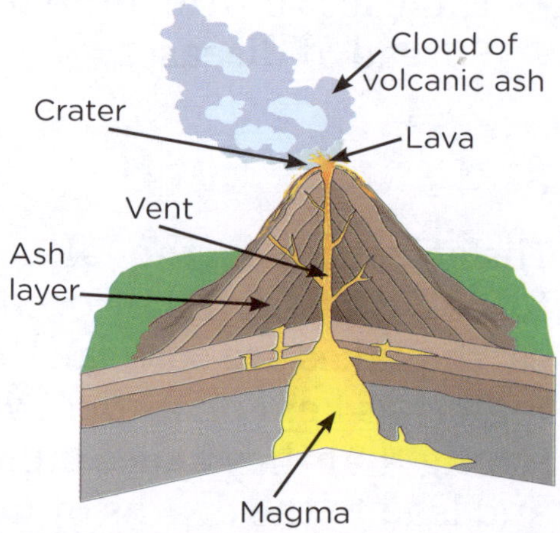

A volcano

A **vent** is the region where the Earth's crust is weak and develops a crack. Once hot magma comes out of the Earth's surface, it is called **lava**. After a volcanic eruption occurs, a crater is formed at the region of the vent.

Volcanoes are of three types, depending on how frequently they erupt: active, dormant and extinct.

**Active volcanoes:** These are considered to be highly dangerous. They may erupt at any time, or have erupted in recent years. Some of the most active volcanoes are Mount St. Helens in the United States, Mount Mayon in the Philippines, and Mount Lassen in the United States.

**Dormant volcanoes:** Volcanoes that have not erupted for a long period but may erupt in the future are called dormant volcanoes. Some of the dormant volcanoes are Mauna Kea in Hawaii, Mount Edziza in Canada and Narcondam in the Andaman Islands of India.

**Extinct volcanoes:** Volcanoes that are not expected to erupt in the future are called extinct volcanoes. Some of the extinct volcanoes are Mount Ashitaka in Japan, Shiprock in the United States and Zuidwal in the Netherlands.

## After-effects of Volcanic Eruptions

1. Destruction of farmlands and roads, damage to property and the loss of life.
2. Volcanic dust blocks sunlight for a long period, which leads to the change in the weather pattern.
3. Spread of diseases

**Wonder!**

A region in the Pacific ocean that consists of 452 volcanoes is called **the ring of fire**.

## Advantages of Volcanic Eruptions

1. After a volcanic eruption, the soil becomes very fertile and good for farming.
2. Some of the volcanic locations can be used to generate geothermal energy[1].

**Word Web**

[1]**Geothermal energy:** energy obtained from the Earth

# TIDAL WAVES AND TSUNAMIS

Tides are the cyclic rise and fall of the sea levels caused due to the gravitational pull of the sun and the moon. At times, the waves on the sea are high, and some times they are low. Tides reach their maximum height when the sun, the moon and the Earth are in a straight line.

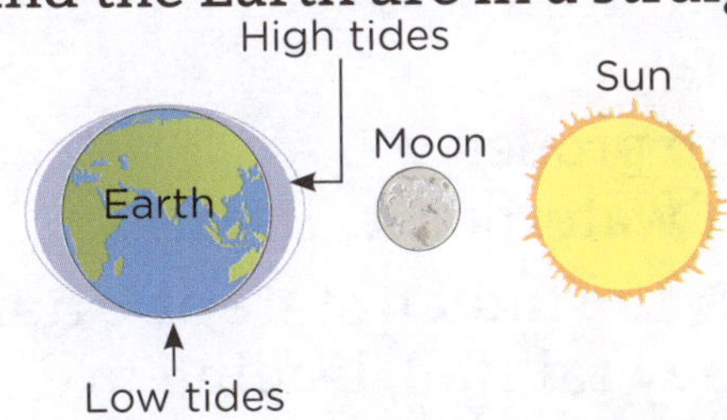


Rise of large amount of water in the form of huge waves from oceans due to underwater earthquakes, volcanic eruptions, etc., is called **tsunami**. When there is a disturbance in the layers of rocks in the Earth's crust under water bodies, a large amount of energy is released, which leads to the formation of huge waves. Large tsunami waves lead to the loss of both life and property. It is advisable to stay at high altitude regions during a tsunami threat.

Tsunami waves

On 26 December 2004, a tsunami occurred in the Indian Ocean, causing a major loss of life and property in the coastal regions of Tamil Nadu and Kerala. The Andaman and Nicobar islands were among the worst hit areas in India.

# FLOODS

Flood

Approximately 75% of the Earth's surface is covered by water. When water bodies, such as the oceans, rivers, lakes and ponds, have excess water, they overflow leading to floods.

Floods occur due to the following natural factors:

- Heavy rainfall
- Low-pressure region formed in the ocean
- Excess melting of the snow in mountains and glaciers

Floods can be prevented by taking the following measures:

- Constructing proper streams or channels for the excess water to flow through
- Planting enough trees to slow down the force with which the water flows
- Constructing proper embankments[1] that control the level of water flowing into the rivers

## After-effects of Floods

- Loss of life
- Damage to property
- Spread of waterborne diseases

**Word Web**

[1]**Embankment:** a wall made of mud and stone to keep water back

In June 2013, the Indian state of Uttarakhand and nearby places received heavy rainfall, leading to devastating floods and landslides. It caused heavy damage to life and property.

## Safety Measures During Floods

Some safety measures you can take to be safe during a flood are given below:

- Do not panic. Always listen to flood warnings given on the radio and news channels.
- Leave the area where the flood water is bound to flow.
- Shift to higher locations where the flood water cannot reach.
- Keep plenty of medicines, food supplies, water purifiers and clean drinking water.
- Follow instructions given by the rescue team workers.

## DROUGHT

Drought is a condition or the state of severe shortage of water supply (both surface and underground). Some droughts are of shorter duration, whereas some continue for years.

Droughts occur due to a lack of, or insufficient rainfall, along with the excessive usage of existing water resources.

Drought

### Effects of drought

Some effects of droughts are as follows:

- Destruction of crops
- Malnutrition and death of humans and animals
- Mass movement of people from one place to another

The effects of a drought can be controlled by taking the following steps:

- Making judicious[1] usage of the available water resources
- Adapting to rainwater harvesting
- Recycling of water
- Cultivating crops that require less water

Major drought-prone regions in India include Southern and Eastern Maharashtra, Northern Karnataka, Andhra Pradesh, Odisha, Gujarat and Rajasthan.

In 2012, the Indian state of Karnataka faced severe drought.

**Word Web**

[1]**Judicious:** careful and sensible

**Science in Context**

Drip irrigation is a modern irrigation technique that saves water. It is done by using narrow tubes that allow a very small quantity of water to drip into the roots of plants.

### Revise and Recall

**Match the following.**

| | |
|---|---|
| 1. Earthquake | (a) Lava |
| 2. Volcano | (b) Insufficient rainfall |
| 3. Huge wave | (c) Epicenter |
| 4. Drought | (d) Embankment |
| 5. Flood | (e) Tsunami |

## Keywords

**Earthquake:** The sudden movement of a part of the Earth's surface

**Volcano:** A crack or vent on the Earth's surface that allows hot magma from below the surface to come out

**Tide:** The cyclic rise and fall of sea the levels caused by the gravitational pull of the sun and the moon

**Tsunami:** Rise of a large amount of water in the form of huge waves from the oceans, due to underwater earthquakes, volcanic eruptions, etc.

**Drought:** A state of a severe shortage of water supply (both surface and underground)

**Flood:** A natural disaster caused by the overflow of oceans, rivers, etc., due to excess water

## Summary

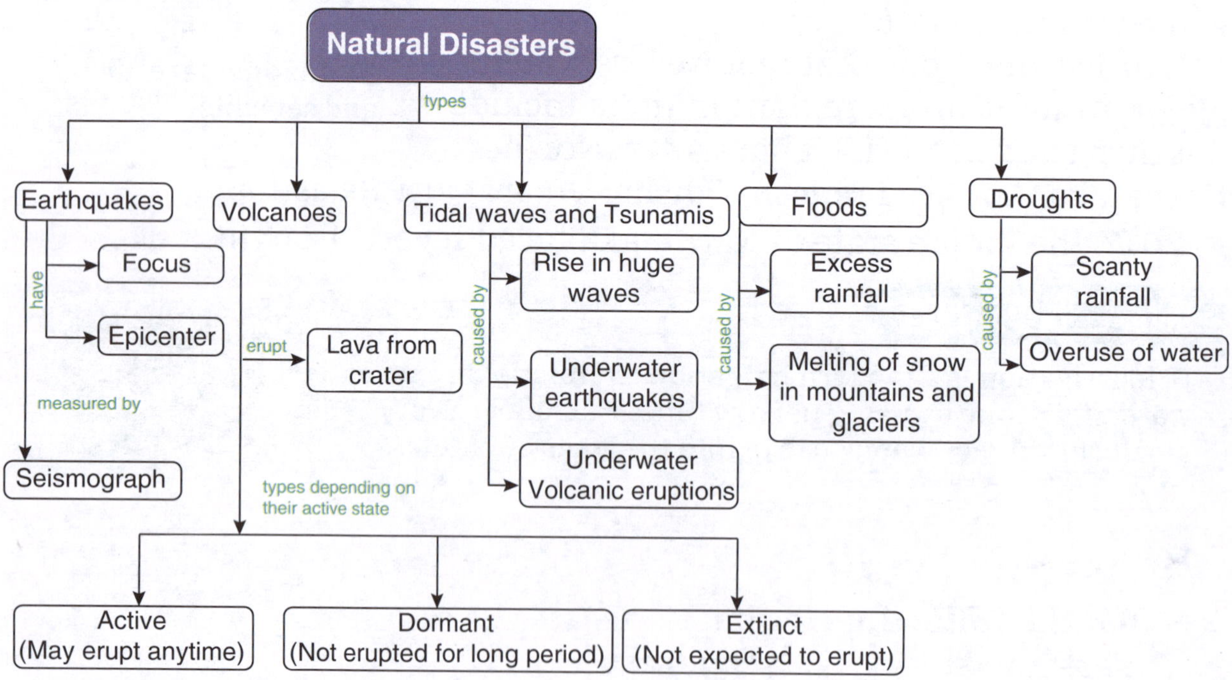

# Exercise

W

**A. Choose the correct option for each of the following.** ia

1. Which of the following natural disasters is caused by disturbances in the Earth's crust?
   (a) Earthquake (b) Flood (c) Tide (d) Drought
2. The actual point deep in the Earth's crust where an earthquake begins is called ____________.
   (a) mantle (b) core (c) focus (d) epicentre
3. Which volcanoes are capable of erupting?
   (a) Dormant and active (b) Active and extinct
   (c) Extinct and dormant (d) Active, dormant and extinct
4. Which of the following natural disasters is caused by the shortage of water?
   (a) Drought (b) Tsunami (c) Earthquake (d) Volcanic eruption
5. Heavy rainfall can cause ____________.
   (a) earthquake (b) drought
   (c) volcanic eruption (d) flood

**B. State whether the following statements are true (T) or false (F).** ia

1. Tides are formed due to the gravitational pull of the sun and the moon.
2. Drought occurs when water bodies overflow due to excess water.
3. The effect of an earthquake is felt more at the epicentre.
4. Tides and tsunami are one and the same.
5. When magma comes out of the Earth's surface, it is called lava.

**C. Fill in the blanks using the correct words.** ia

1. The innermost layer of the Earth is called ____________. (core/mantle)
2. The magnitude of an earthquake is measured using the ____________. (seismograph/Richter scale)
3. Volcanoes that erupt frequently are called ____________ volcanoes. (active/extinct)
4. Floods occur due to ____________ water. (excess/lack of)
5. Earthquake measuring ____________ on the Richter scale is considered to be highly dangerous. (3/8)

**D. Name the following.**

1. The point on the Earth where an earthquake begins
2. Huge waves formed due to an earthquake occurring underwater
3. The instrument used to measure the intensity and duration of earthquakes
4. The region where the Earth's crust is weak and develops a crack
5. The natural disaster that occurs due to the lack of rainfall

**E. Give reasons for the following.**

1. Active volcanoes are highly dangerous.
2. Rainwater harvesting can reduce the effect of drought.
3. Volcanic locations can be used to generate geothermal energy.
4. Earthquakes under water lead to Tsunami.
5. Excessive melting of glaciers will lead to loss of life.

**F. Answer the following questions briefly.**

1. What is an earthquake?
2. What is an epicentre?
3. What is a dormant volcano?
4. What causes tides?
5. What is a tsunami?

**G. Answer the following questions.**

1. What are the after-effects of an earthquake? Give three safety measures to be followed during earthquakes.
2. What is a volcano? Explain different types of volcanoes with one example each.
3. Write two after-effects and two advantages of volcanic eruption.
4. When do floods occur? What are the after-effects of flood?
5. Give the measures that can be taken to prevent or reduce the effects of drought.

# Cognitive Corner

## Critical Thinking

1. Amit is on the first floor of a building. If an earthquake occurs suddenly, which method is better for him to come out of the building: by using the stairs or the elevator? Why?
2. Can an earthquake cause a tsunami? Explain.

## Picture Study

Label the parts of the volcano as shown below.

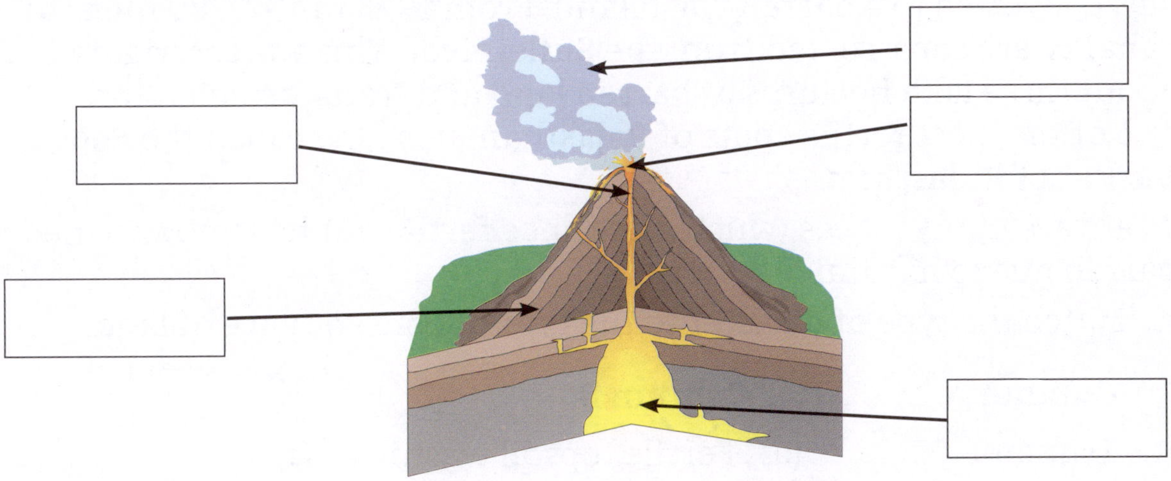

## Project

Search the Internet or newspapers with the help of an elder and make a report on natural disasters. Cover the following points:

- Name of the disaster
- The date on which it occured
- Places affected by the disaster
- Details of damage or loss of life caused, if available

## Life Skills

List the things and supplies that might be essential to carry during a natural disaster. What type of bag would you prefer to carry the essentials?

# Worksheet

India is a land with mountains, seas, rivers, plains and deserts. The state of Rajasthan mainly comprises deserts.

Do you think it is possible to change a wasteland into a productive one?

Let us do a case study.

A desert

Sri Ganganagar is a city in the northern Rajasthan. In ancient times, this area was watered by two major rivers. However, in course of time, the rivers dried up and the land was converted to a barren wasteland. From 1925 to 1927, 89 miles of canals were constructed from the Sutlej river. This water irrigated about three lakh hectares of barren land and transformed it into one of the most fertile spots of Rajasthan. It is now called the **Food Basket of Rajasthan**.

There are many places which were once fertile but have now turned barren due to natural disasters.

A. Match the type of disaster to the type of consequence of land.

| | **Column A** | | **Column B** |
|---|---|---|---|
| 1. | Tsunami | (a) | Fertile topsoil washing off |
| 2. | Flood | (b) | Land drying up |
| 3. | Drought | (c) | Irrigated land getting salty from seawater |

B. Find out about any one place in India which is changed from a barren land to fertile land due to human efforts. If possible, collect pictures of that place and paste them in the space given below.

# 10 Rocks and Minerals

## Learning Checklist

- Types of rocks
- Minerals
- Uses of rocks and minerals

## Let's Get Started

Look at the pictures given below and fill in the blanks with the given words.

Chalk    Ruby    Granite

________________ is used to make kitchen slabs.

________________ is used to write on blackboards.

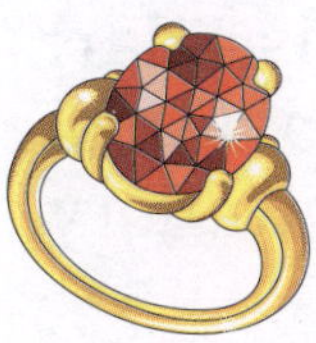

________________ is used in making jewellery.

Rocks are the hard part of the Earth's crust. They break down to form soil. Rocks and minerals are of different shapes, sizes and colours. They are found everywhere on the Earth. Let us learn more about them.

# TYPES OF ROCKS

A volcanic eruption

Rocks can be divided into three groups based on how they are formed: igneous, sedimentary and metamorphic.

## Igneous Rocks

We have learned in Chapter 9 that the core of the Earth is made of molten rock called **magma**. When magma comes out to the surface of the Earth through volcanic eruptions, it is called **lava**.

The lava cools down and hardens to form igneous rocks. Some of the minerals present in igneous rocks are mica, feldspar, magnesium and quartz. Igneous rocks derive their name from the Latin word *ignis*, which means 'fiery'.

Granite, pumice and obsidian are the examples of igneous rocks.

**Granite** is formed due to the slow cooling of lava. The three main minerals found in granite are mica, feldspar and quartz. The colour of granite varies from grey to pink, based on the amount of feldspar present. Granite is used to make buildings, kitchen interiors, floorings, etc.

**Pumice** is formed by the rapid cooling of lava. It is creamish or grey in colour. The release of gases from the lava forms the pores in the pumice rock.

Unlike other rocks, pumice is lightweight. It is used in making lightweight building materials, footscrubs, etc.

**Science in Context**

Pieces of pumice rocks can float on water, because the air-pores present in them make them less dense than water.

**Obsidian** is also formed due to the rapid cooling of lava. It is a dark or black-coloured rock. It is smooth and glassy; hence, it is also called **volcanic glass**. It has very sharp edges. It is used to make jewellery.

Granite

Pumice

Obsidian

Igneous rocks

## Sedimentary Rocks

Sedimentary rocks are formed due to the deposition of small pieces of rock, soil, and plant and animal matter over thousands of years, by the action of wind, rainwater and flowing river water.

**Science in Context**

Coal and petroleum are always found in sedimentary rocks. Coal is formed from the buried remains of forests. Petroleum is formed from the remains of plants and animals buried in the sea.

Rivers flowing down a mountain wear away rocks. Wind and rainwater also wear away rocks. These small pieces of rocks are deposited at some other place. Layer over layer is deposited over a long period of time. This repeated deposition hardens the lower layers, leading to the formation of sedimentary rocks.

Conglomerate, sandstone, shale and limestone are some of the examples of sedimentary rocks.

**Conglomerate** contains gravel, round pebbles and boulders, held together by minerals. It has an uneven texture and is used as a building material.

**Limestone** contains the mineral calcium along with tiny animal shells. Its grains are soft and fine. It is used to make lime, cement, paint, etc.

**Sandstone** is formed by the deposition of sand particles held together by minerals such as silica. Famous Indian monuments, such as the Red Fort and the Qutub Minar, are made of sandstone.

**Shale** contains solidified clay and mud, piled up in layers. It is used to make construction materials, such as bricks, tiles and cement.

Conglomerate

Limestone

Sandstone

Shale

Sedimentary rocks

## Metamorphic Rocks

**Metamorphism** means a gradual change in form. Igneous rocks and sedimentary rocks change into metamorphic rocks over time, due to both high pressure and temperature.

Slate, marble, quartzite and gneiss are some examples of metamorphic rocks.

**Slate** is formed from the sedimentary rock, shale. Slate mainly contains clay, mica and other minerals. It can be broken into thin layers. It is used to make slates for children, blackboards for classrooms as well as cement.

**Marble** is formed from the sedimentary rock limestone. It has been widely used for the purpose of construction from the ancient times. One of the best examples of this is the Taj Mahal in Agra, which is made of white marble. Marble is also used in making flooring material and statues.

**Quartzite** is formed from the sedimentary rock sandstone. It mainly contains iron, quartz and silica. These are hard rocks, and are not easily broken. It is used to make floorings and stairs, and in the glass and ceramic industries.

**Gneiss** is formed from the igneous rock granite. It has light and dark bands of varying length and thickness. It is used as a building material.

Slate

Marble

Quartzite

Gneiss

Metamorphic rocks

## Revise and Recall

**Match the following.**

| Column A | Column B |
|---|---|
| 1. Taj Mahal is made of | (a) Obsidian |
| 2. Molten rock inside the Earth's core | (b) Sandstone |
| 3. Lightweight rock with holes | (c) Marble |
| 4. The rock used in building Red Fort | (d) Magma |
| 5. Volcanic glass | (e) Pumice |

## MINERALS

a

Rocks are made up of substances called minerals. Minerals are formed inside the Earth.

There are two types of minerals: metallic and non-metallic.

**Metallic Minerals:** These minerals yield metals. Metal-yielding minerals are also called **ores**. A few examples of ores are bauxite, pyrite and hematite. These ores can be processed to obtain aluminium, copper and iron, respectively.

Metals are used in making machines, cars, ships, wires, etc. Gold, silver and platinum are precious metals that are used to make both jewellery and ornaments.

Gold

Iron bars used in construction

Copper

Metals obtained from minerals

**Non-metallic Minerals:** Some important non-metallic minerals are coal, salt, gypsum, mica and feldspar.

Coal is used in the thermal power generation, for cooking, and in other industries where a large amount of heat is required.

Coal

Emerald (a gemstone)

Non-metallic minerals

**Gemstones** are also obtained from minerals. Pieces of these minerals are cut and polished and then used to make jewellery. These gemstones are found in very attractive colours, such as red, green and yellow.

A few examples of gemstones are diamond, ruby, sapphire and emerald. These are also known as precious stones.

**Science in Context**

Diamond is the hardest mineral and can withstand very high temperatures.

## USES OF ROCKS AND MINERALS

Rocks and minerals have been used by human beings from ancient times. Even to this day, we use products obtained from them.

These are some of the most common uses of rocks and minerals.

**Construction:** We use rocks and stones for building houses, offices, etc. Stones and jelly stones are used all through the building process. Even the cement used in the construction of buildings is derived from minerals. Tar is used to make roads, while marbles are used for flooring. Iron and steel are used to make pillars for buildings.

**Metals:** Utensils are the basic requirements of a kitchen in a home. These are made from iron, copper, aluminium and steel. All these are made or obtained from mineral ores.

Metals such as gold, silver and platinum are used to make ornaments, decorative items and jewellery.

**Gemstones:** Gemstones such as diamond, ruby, sapphire and emerald are used to make jewellery.

**Fuels:** Coal is used as a fuel to keep homes warm in colder regions and for cooking. Uranium is a rare mineral. It is used in nuclear reactors to produce large amounts of energy.

Petroleum is a liquid mineral. It is called black gold because of its commercial value. Various products, such as kerosene, diesel, cooking gas and lubricants, are all produced from petroleum. Coal is used to produce chemicals which are used in perfumes, plastics, cloth dyes and nylon.

**Fertilizers:** Minerals such as sulphates and nitrates are constituents of fertilizers. Fertilizers are added to the soil to increase the fertility of soil, thereby increasing the yield of crops.

**Food:** We use rock salt (*kala namak*) in food. It is obtained from the rocks in the Earth.

Many other minerals, such as calcium, iron and potassium, are required for the growth and development of our body. We get these from the vegetables and fruits we eat. Plants obtain these minerals from the soil.

The following table lists some of the minerals and their use in our daily lives:

| Minerals | Used in |
|---|---|
| Quartz | Watches |
| Talc | Talcum or face powder |
| Graphite | Pencils |
| Diamond | Jewellery |
| Copper | Electrical wires |
| Mica | Welding rods, electronic goods |

## Keywords

**Crust:** The outer surface of the Earth on which we live

**Magma:** Molten rock present inside the Earth

**Lava:** Magma flowing on the surface of the Earth after a volcanic eruption

**Igneous rocks:** Rocks formed as a result of the cooling and solidification of molten rock

**Sedimentary rocks:** Rocks formed due to the deposition of small pieces of rock, soil, and plant and animal matter carried by the wind or flowing water

**Metamorphic rocks:** Rocks formed when igneous or sedimentary rocks undergo changes over a period of time

**Ore:** Metal-yielding minerals

## Summary

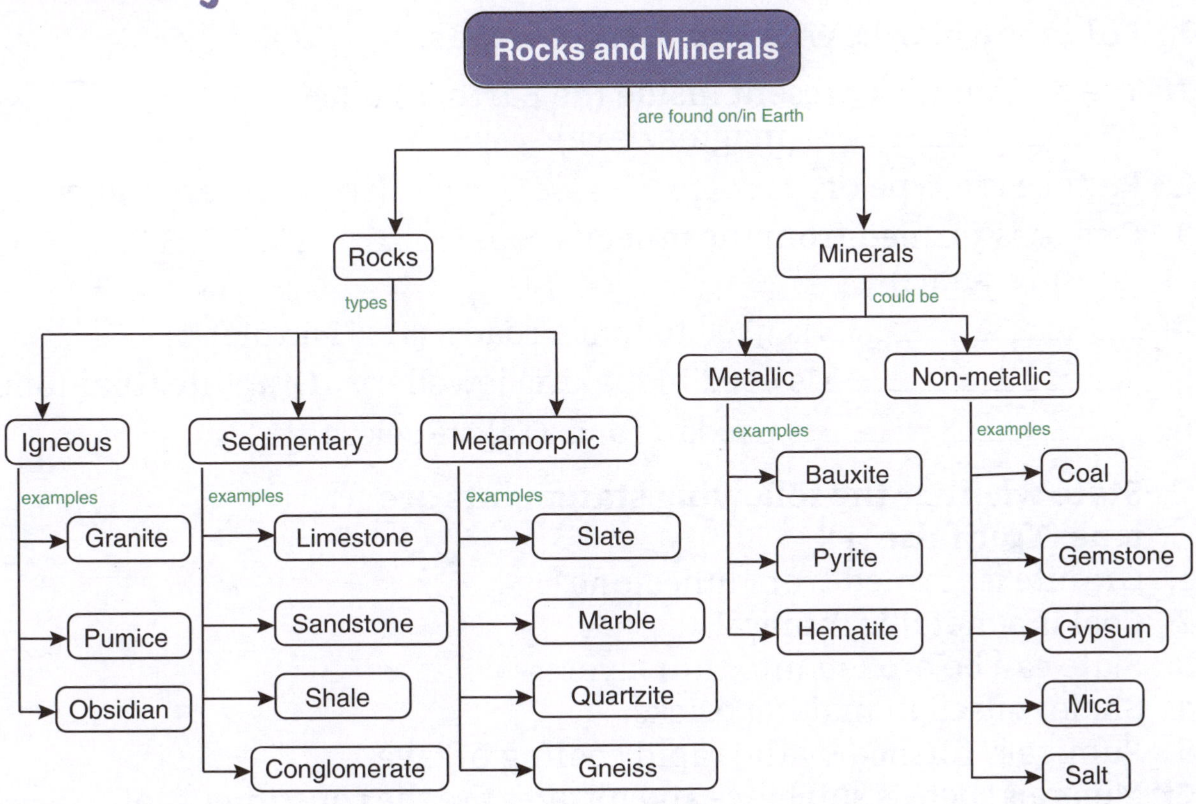

# Exercise

W

**A. Choose the correct option for each of the following.** ia

1. Which of the following is an igneous rock?
   (a) Obsidian (b) Sandstone (c) Limestone (d) Slate
2. A sedimentary rock that contains solidified mud and clay piled up in layers is ______________.
   (a) limestone (b) sandstone (c) shale (d) conglomerate
3. ______________ is the metamorphic rock formed from sandstone.
   (a) Gneiss (b) Marble (c) Quartzite (d) Slate
4. Which of the following is a non-metallic mineral?
   (a) Pyrite (b) Bauxite (c) Hematite (d) Gypsum
5. Which of the following is a gemstone?
   (a) Coal (b) Mica (c) Emerald (d) Feldspar
6. Which of the following minerals is used to make welding rods and electrical goods?
   (a) Talc (b) Mica (c) Quartz (d) Diamond

**B. Fill in the blanks with the correct words.** ia

1. The molten rock present inside the Earth is called ______________. (magma/lava)
2. Pumice is a type of ______________ rock. (sedimentary/igneous)
3. Gneiss is formed from the igneous rock ______________. (granite/shale)
4. ______________ is used to make roads. (Tar/Marble)
5. ______________ is used in making jewellery. (Graphite/Diamond)
6. ______________ is used in food. (Talc/Rock salt)

**C. State whether the following statements are true (T) or false (F).** ia

1. Granite is formed from limestone.
2. Coal is a metallic mineral.
3. Slate can be broken into thin layers.
4. Shale is used in making bricks.
5. Pumice is formed by the rapid cooling of lava.
6. Minerals such as sulphates and nitrates are the constituents of fertilizers.

**D. Give one example for each of the following.**

1. Igneous rock
2. Mineral
3. Gemstone
4. Metamorphic rock
5. Sedimentary rock

**E. Match the following.**

| Column A | Column B |
|---|---|
| 1. Igneous | (a) Marble |
| 2. Sedimentary | (b) Feldspar |
| 3. Metamorphic | (c) Obsidian |
| 4. Non-metallic mineral | (d) Diamond |
| 5. Gemstone | (e) Conglomerate |

**F. Give reasons for the following.**

1. Petroleum is called black gold.
2. It takes a long period of time to form metamorphic rocks.
3. Fossils are seen mostly in sedimentary rocks.
4. Some minerals are also used as fertilizers.
5. Pumice floats on water.

**G. Answer the following questions in brief.**

1. Which types of rocks are formed after a volcanic eruption? Give two examples.
2. Which rock is also called volcanic glass? Give one use of this rock.
3. What are the two things that help in the formation of sedimentary rocks?
4. What are the two constituents of sandstone? Name two monuments made of sandstone.
5. What are metamorphic rocks? Give two examples.
6. What are minerals? Name the two types of minerals.
7. What are gemstones? What are they used for?
8. What are ores? Give two examples.

**H. Answer the following questions.**

1. Explain the formation of igneous rocks.
2. Explain the formation of sedimentary rocks. Give two examples and explain their features.

3. Explain the features of metamorphic rocks and their formation.
4. Describe the rock quartzite.
5. Give the various uses of rocks and minerals.

# Cognitive Corner

## Critical Thinking

1. Romila says gold and silver are metals, but Lekha says they are minerals. Who is correct? Can both be correct? Why or why not?
2. Why are igneous rocks called primary rocks?

## Picture Study

Name the rocks the following monuments are made of.

Red Fort

_______________

Taj Mahal

_______________

## Project

Collect stones of different colours and identify them with the help of your teacher. Keep them in egg trays and make an exhibit for your school science exhibition.

## Life Skills

All the minerals are exhaustible, that is, the availability of these minerals is limited.

Discuss the following in your class.

- What are the difficulties that we would have to face if minerals get exhausted in nature?
- How can we help to save minerals for the future?

# Worksheet

The Earth's outer layer is mainly made of rocks and soil. The soil forms a thin layer on top of a thick rocky layer. These rocks are considered non-living. However, there are rocks that are living. These living rocks are called corals. These amazing rocks are found in various parts of the world under the sea.

Corals

Corals are a class of sea animals which have a hard, outer shell. These animals live in colonies. When these animals die, their shells remain there. Over a long period of time, these shells become hard and resemble rocks. These rocks are very colourful and are a great attraction for tourists from around the world. Pollution of oceans and seas have caused a great danger to these coral rocks.

A. Look at the pictures given below and identify two reasons that pollute oceans.

____________________ ____________________

B. Make a poster on 'SAVE THE LIVING ROCKS' and colour it.

# 11 Solids, Liquids and Gases

## Learning Checklist

- What is matter made up of?
- Heating and cooling of solids, liquids and gases
- Physical and chemical changes

## Let's Get Started

We know that water exists in three different forms or states: solid, liquid and gas. Draw a line to match the pictures on the left with those on the right that show the same state of matter.

1. 

(a) 

2. 

(b) 

3. 

(c) 

Everything in the universe is made up of matter. A substance that has mass and occupies space is called **matter**. Matter can exist in three states: solid, liquid and gas. It is made up of small particles called **atoms** and **molecules**. Let us learn more about them.

# WHAT IS MATTER MADE UP OF?

**Atoms** are the building blocks of all matter. They are extremely small in size and can be seen only with the help of very powerful microscopes. Though you cannot see them with the naked eye, everything around you is made up of atoms. The water you drink, the air you breathe, the Earth and everything on it is made up of atoms.

## Molecules

$O_2$
Oxygen molecule

$H_2O$
Water molecule

When two or more atoms combine together, they form a particle called a **molecule**. A molecule can be made up of the same or different kind of atoms. For example, an oxygen molecule is made up of two oxygen atoms (also written as $O_2$), whereas a water molecule is made up of two hydrogen atoms and one oxygen atom (also written as $H_2O$).

Atoms and molecules are in constant motion, that is, they are always moving. In **solids**, the atoms or the molecules move, but remain in the same position. In other words, they only vibrate without changing their position. That is why, solids have a fixed shape. In **liquids**, the atoms or the molecules move around and glide over each other. That is why, liquids flow easily and can be poured into containers. In **gases**, the atoms or the molecules move freely and are not in contact with each other. That is why, gases move to take up the entire space available to them.

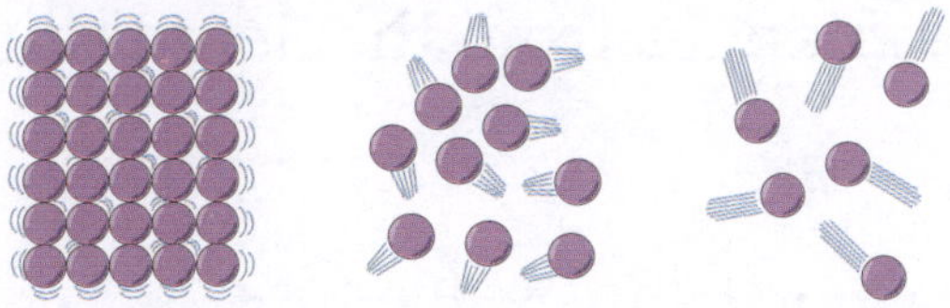

(a) (b) (c)

Movement of particles in
(a) solids (b) liquids and (c) gases

**Science in Context**

**Nanotechnology** is the branch of science that involves working with atoms and molecules to build devices (such as robots) that are extremely small.

## Intermolecular Space

The space between two molecules is called their **intermolecular space**.

The molecules are held together by a force of attraction, which is very strong in solids, weaker in liquids and very weak in gases.

A spoon of sugar added to water dissolves in it because the sugar molecules occupy the intermolecular space in water.

Some liquids, such as alcohol, also dissolve in water. Gases, such as oxygen and carbon dioxide, dissolve in water. Fish breathe in the oxygen dissolved in water.

**Science in Context**

The lightness or heaviness of a substance for a given volume is called density. Density depends on how closely the molecules are packed in a given substance. Thus, a stone is denser than a block of wood, because the particles in a stone are very closely packed compared to a block of wood. Density of water (1 g/cc) is taken as a standard for measurement of density of liquids.

**Wonder!**

Have you ever wondered which is heavier—1 kg of iron or 1 kg of cotton? You may say iron, but this is not true, as both weigh the same. The difference is in the intermolecular space between the two. The particles of iron are very closely packed, making the iron ball denser. The particles of cotton, on the other hand, are loosely packed. So, it occupies more space, but is less dense.

## HEATING AND COOLING OF LIQUIDS

What happens when we heat a liquid?

When a liquid is heated, the molecules acquire energy and move faster. When it is heated continuously, the molecules ultimately move so fast that they are no longer in contact with each other, and thus, the liquid changes into gas.

This process in which a liquid changes into gas is called **evaporation**. Evaporation causes wet clothes to dry, and the water in them to disappear (that is, water in the clothes changes from the liquid state to gaseous state).

What happens when we cool a liquid?

When a liquid is cooled, the molecules slow down, and when the cooling is continued, the molecules come close together and rearrange themselves to become a solid. This process in which a liquid changes into a solid is called **freezing**. The rate of freezing is different for different liquids.

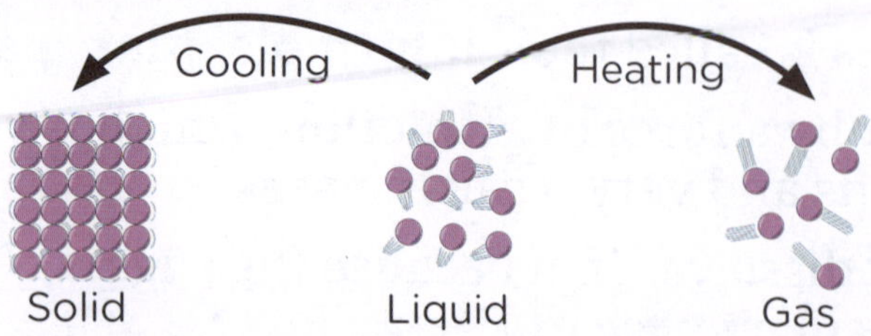


**Science in Context**

Ice formed by freezing of water is less dense than water. Hence, ice floats on water.

## HEATING AND COOLING OF SOLIDS

When solids are heated, the molecules start to vibrate faster. On further heating, the particles move around and gradually turn into a liquid.

This process, in which a solid changes into liquid, is called **melting**. Not all substances undergo melting at normal conditions. Some solid substances may undergo certain other changes on heating. For example, paper burns when it is heated. However, most solids expand on heating.

Let us understand this concept from the example given below.

Safeena has a metal ball and a ring. Before heating the metal ball, the ball could pass through the ring. Then, she heated the metal ball over a flame until it got very hot. She tried to pass the heated metal ball through the ring and found that the ball could not pass through the ring.

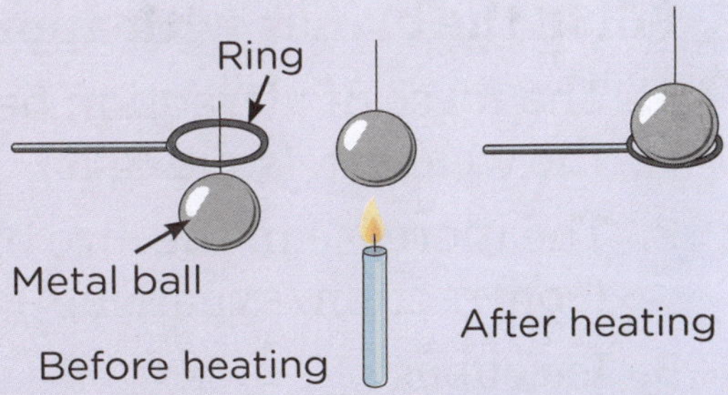


- What would Safeena conclude from this experiment?
- How can Safeena pass the metal ball through the ring once again?

In the above example, when the ball is heated, the molecules move further apart, causing the size of the ball to increase. This is called **expansion**[1].

When the ball is cooled, the movement of the molecules slows down, and they come closer to each other. This is called **contraction**[2].

**Word Web**

[1]**Expansion:** increase in the size of matter

[2]**Contraction:** decrease in the size of matter

## HEATING AND COOLING OF GASES

When a gas is heated, the molecules move away very fast, thereby causing it to expand. When a gas is cooled for a long time, the molecules slow down and the gas gradually turns into a liquid. This process, in which a gas changes into liquid, is called **condensation**.

**Science in Context**

A gas expands faster than a solid or a liquid, because the force of attraction between the particles of a gas is the weakest.

The formation of water droplets on the outer surface of a cold glass is an example of condensation.

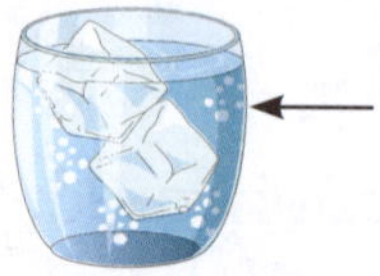


When the water vapour present in the air comes in contact with the cold surface of the glass, the movement of molecules in water vapour slows down. Hence, water vapour (gas) turns into water (liquid). Formation of dew and mist are other examples of condensation.

## Revise and Recall

**Fill in the blanks with appropriate answers.**

1. The force of attraction between the particles of ____________ is the weakest. (solid/gas)
2. The increase in the size of matter is known as ____________. (contraction/expansion)
3. Ice cubes ____________ when heated. (melt/condense)
4. When water is heated, it undergoes ______. (evaporation/freezing)

## Activity

**Aim:** To show that air expands on heating and contracts on cooling

**Materials required:** A balloon, a 2-litre water bottle, a bowl of hot water and a bowl of cold water

Bottle with balloon in hot water

Bottle with balloon in cold water

**Procedure:**

1. Fix a slightly inflated balloon to the mouth of the 2-litre bottle.
2. Place the bottle with the balloon into the bowl of hot water. Observe the change.
3. Place the bottle with the balloon into bowl of cold water and observe the change.

**Observation:** The balloon gets inflated when the bottle is kept in hot water. The balloon gets deflated when the bottle is kept in cold water.

**Reason:** The hot water heats up the air inside the bottle. The air expands and inflates the balloon. In the bowl of cold water, the air inside the bottle gets cooled and contracts. This causes the balloon to deflate.

**Conclusion:** Air expands on heating and contracts on cooling.

## Keywords

**Atoms:** Building blocks of all matter

**Molecules:** Particles formed when two or more atoms combine

**Evaporation:** The process in which a liquid changes into gas

**Condensation:** The process in which a gas changes into liquid

## Summary

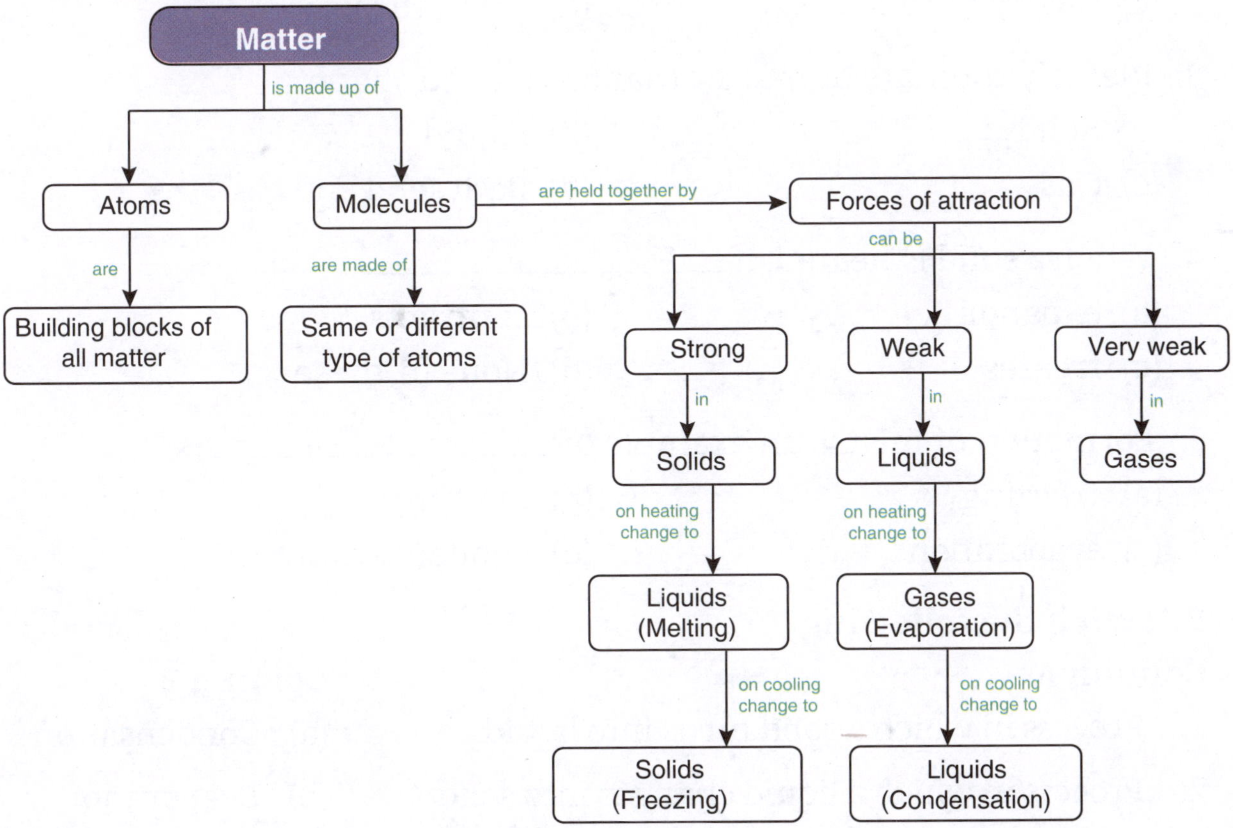

# Exercise

W

ia

**A. Choose the correct option for each of the following.**

1. Matter has mass and occupies ____________________.
   (a) weight  (b) space
   (c) energy  (d) None of these
2. Identify the state of matter in which the molecules spread out and occupy the entire space available.
   (a) Solid  (b) Liquid
   (c) Gas  (d) All of these
3. Identify the state of matter that has a fixed shape.
   (a) Solid  (b) Liquid
   (c) Gas  (d) Both solid and gas
4. When a solid is heated, it ____________________.
   (a) expands  (b) contracts
   (c) freezes  (d) None of these
5. Formation of mist is an example of ____________________.
   (a) freezing  (b) melting
   (c) evaporation  (d) condensation

**B. Match the following.**

ia

| **Column A** | **Column B** |
|---|---|
| 1. Process in which a solid turns into liquid | (a) Condensation |
| 2. Process in which a liquid changes into solid | (b) Evaporation |
| 3. Process in which a liquid changes into gas | (c) Freezing |
| 4. Process in which a gas changes into liquid | (d) Melting |

**C. State whether the following statements are true (T) or false (F).**

1. Atoms are the building blocks of matter.
2. Molecules are made up of only the same kind of atoms.

3. When heated, atoms move faster.
4. All substances undergo melting in normal conditions.
5. Solids expand on heating.

**D. Give reasons for the following.**

1. A tablespoon of salt dissolves in a glass of water.
2. Some solids expand on heating.
3. Droplets of water are seen on the surface of a cold tumbler.
4. In gases, molecules move freely.
5. An iron ball feels heavier than a cotton ball of the same weight.

**E. Answer the following in one word.** ia

1. A substance that occupies space and has mass
2. Building block of matter
3. The state of matter in which particles move freely
4. The space between two molecules
5. An example of a liquid

**F. Answer the following questions briefly.**

1. Why is a molecule of oxygen written as $O_2$?
2. What is the difference between melting and freezing?
3. What happens when a solid is heated?
4. What happens to the particles when a gas is cooled?
5. What is expansion?

**G. Answer the following questions.**

1. Do solids expand on heating? Justify your statement with the help of an activity.
2. Explain what happens when a liquid is heated and cooled.
3. Differentiate between an atom and a molecule with an example.

# Cognitive Corner

## Critical Thinking

1. When someone opens a bottle of perfume in one corner of a room, we can smell it from the other corner. Why?
2. Ronak heated three glass bottles half-filled with water, ice cubes and the other empty and fitted each with a rubber cork. Which bottle would have popped the cork first? Why?

## Picture Study

Sketch to show how water would look like in each of the containers shown below.

Did the shape of water stay the same or did it change in each of the containers?

## Project

1. Collect pictures of the different items found in your household and paste them in your scrapbook. Write solid, liquid or gas below each.
2. Draw the arrangement of particles in solids, liquids and gases on a chart paper and display it in your class.

## Life Skills

Keep a half-filled frozen bottle of water at room temperature in a transparent empty bowl. Observe the bowl and bottle after leaving the setup undisturbed for some time.

1. Was the bowl empty after some time?
2. What happened to the water in the bottle after some time?
3. Describe the process of the change of states of matter observed briefly.

# Worksheet

Some objects float on water and some sink. For example, a dry leaf floats on water whereas marbles sink in water. The density of leaf is less than that of water, so it floats on its surface. The density of a marble is more than that of water, so it sinks in it.

A dry leaf

Marbles

A. Suppose you have two similar inflated balls. Release all the air from one of the balls. Now, place both the balls in water. Which ball will float and which will sink?

The inflated ball will ______________ and the deflated ball will ____________.

Why is there a difference? The density of the material of which the ball is made is more than that of water, so the deflated ball sinks. However, in case of the inflated ball, the total density of the ball and the air inside it is less than that of water, so it floats.

B. Explain why an iron nail sinks but enormous ships float on water?

______________________________________________

______________________________________________

C. Mention one more object that also floats like a ship. Explain how it helps us and paste its picture in the box given below.

______________________________

______________________________

______________________________

______________________________

______________________________

______________________________

# 12 Light and Shadow

## Learning Checklist

- Transparent, translucent and opaque materials
- Shadows

## Let's Get Started

We have learned in earlier classes that objects that produce light are called **luminous objects**. They help us to see the non-luminous objects, which do not produce light.

In the picture given below, put a tick mark (✓) against luminous objects and a cross mark (✗) against non-luminous objects in the boxes provided.

Non-luminous objects are made from different materials. Materials can be grouped on the basis of the amount of light they allow to pass through them. Let us understand this with the help of an activity.

### Activity 1

**Aim:** To identify the different types of materials

**Materials required:** A clear (see-through) plastic cover, a sheet of butter paper and an A4 size chart paper

**Procedure:**

1. Take a clear plastic cover, a butter paper and an A4 size chart paper.
2. Ask your friend to stand in front of you.
3. Now, try to see your friend through each—the plastic cover, the butter paper and the chart paper.

**Conclusion:** You will be able to see your friend clearly through the clear plastic cover, partially through the butter paper, and not at all through the chart paper.

## TRANSPARENT, TRANSLUCENT AND OPAQUE MATERIALS

a

Materials that allow light to pass through them completely are called **transparent materials**. Examples of transparent materials are clear glass, clear water and clear plastic sheet.

Materials that allow light to pass through them partially (not completely) are called **translucent materials**. Examples of translucent materials are butter paper, frosted glass and coloured glass.

Clear water (transparent)

Frosted glass (translucent)

### Wonder!

Is mirror a transparent object? It is not, because we cannot see objects on the other side of a mirror, though we can see our own image clearly.

Materials that block light or do not allow light to pass through them are called **opaque materials**. Examples of opaque materials are wood, bag and books.

Bag (opaque)

Book (opaque)

## SHADOWS

a

We know that a shadow is formed when an object is placed in front of a source of light. Let us perform an activity to understand the formation of shadows by transparent, translucent and opaque objects.

### Activity 2

**Aim:** To understand the formation of shadows by transparent, translucent and opaque materials

**Materials required:** A transparent plastic sheet (A4 size), a translucent tracing sheet (A4 size), a cardboard sheet (A4 size), a torch and a screen

**Procedure:**

1. Take the plastic sheet, the tracing sheet, the cardboard sheet and the torch.
2. Hold the objects, one by one, in front of the screen and project the light from the torch onto each object from the opposite side. What do you observe?

**Observation:**

1. You will see that the opaque cardboard sheet blocks the light completely, and hence, forms a clear and dark shadow on the screen.
2. The translucent tracing sheet partially blocks the light, and thus, forms a lighter shadow on the screen.
3. The transparent sheet does not block the light from passing through it, and hence, does not form any shadow.

From the above activity, it is clear that opaque and translucent objects form shadows, whereas transparent objects do not form shadows.

Thus, a **shadow** is a dark region formed by an object when it blocks the path of light. Three things are required for a shadow to form: a light source, an opaque or a translucent object, and a screen (a surface on which the shadow can form).

### Revise and Recall

**Fill in the blanks using the correct words.**

1. Clear glass and clear water are the examples of ______________ materials. (transparent/translucent)
2. Shadow is formed when an object is placed __________ the source of light. (in front of/behind)

3. A shadow is a ______, formed by a translucent or an opaque object blocking light. (dark region/bright region)
4. ______ materials do not form shadows. (Transparent/ Translucent)
5. Materials that do not allow light to pass through them are ______ materials. (translucent/opaque)

## Features of a Shadow

Following are some features of a shadow.

- A shadow is always formed on the opposite side of the light source.
- A shadow shows only the outline of the shape of the object, and not any other details.
- The colour of a shadow does not depend on the colour of the object. Shadows are always dark.
- The size of a shadow depends on the distance of the light source from the object, and also on the distance of the screen from the object.

When the light source is close to the object, or the screen is away from the object, the size of the shadow increases. When the light source is away from the object, or the screen is close to the object, the size of the shadow decreases.

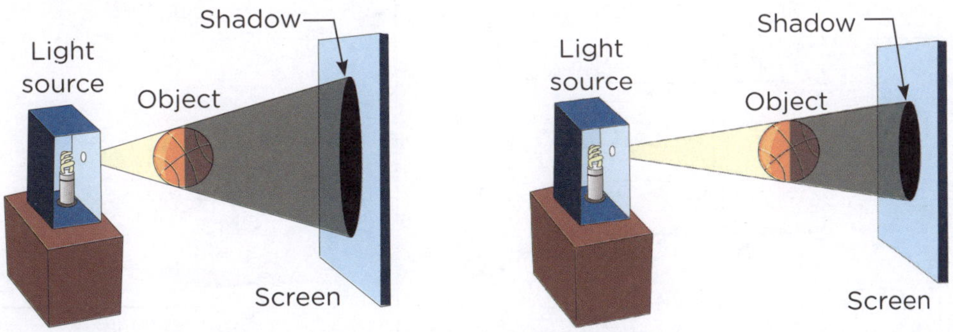


### Science in Context

The shadow of an object is the longest in the morning and evening, and the shortest at noon. This is because the rays of the sun are slanting in the morning and evening, and straight above the head at noon.

## Keywords

**Transparent materials:** Materials that allow light to pass through them completely

**Translucent materials:** Materials that allow light to pass through them partially

**Opaque materials:** Materials that do not allow light to pass through them

**Shadow:** The dark region formed by a translucent or an opaque object when it blocks the path of light

## Summary

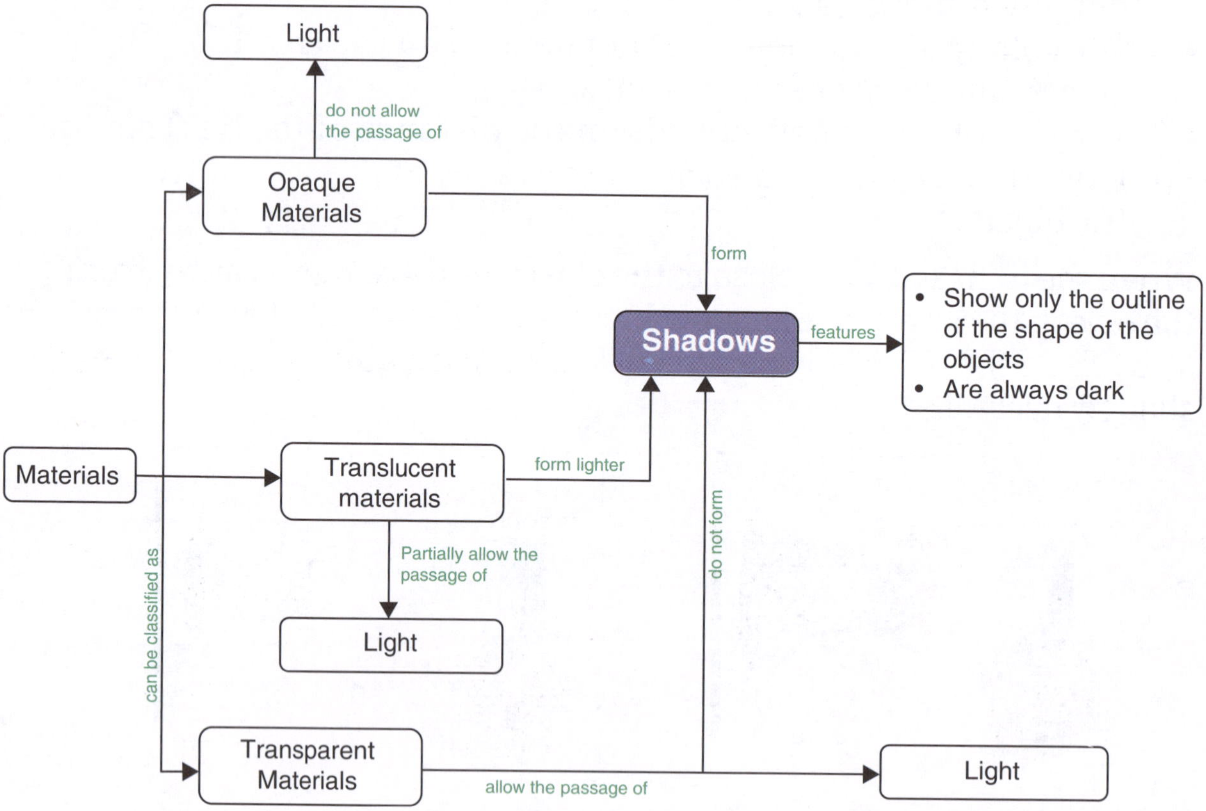

# Exercise

w

**A. Choose the correct option for each of the following.** ia

1. Objects that give out light are called ________.
   (a) non-luminous (b) opaque
   (c) luminous (d) transparent
2. Which of the following is a transparent object?
   (a) Clear glass (b) Wood
   (c) Butter paper (d) Mirror
3. Identify the translucent object from the following.
   (a) Frosted glass (b) Cardboard (c) Mirror (d) Clear water
4. ________ materials do not allow light to pass through them.
   (a) Opaque (b) Transparent (c) Translucent (d) All of these
5. Which of the following objects cannot form a shadow?
   (a) Pencil (b) Clear glass (c) Bag (d) Notebook

**B. State whether the following statements are true (T) or false (F).** ia

1. Translucent materials allow light to pass through them completely.
2. Shadows are always dark.
3. Only transparent materials can form shadows.
4. Shadows can be formed without a light source.
5. The size of the shadow of an object is always the same.

**C. Fill in the blanks using the correct words.** ia

1. A shadow is always formed on the ________ side of the object. (same/opposite)
2. Butter paper is an example of ________ material. (transparent/translucent)
3. Shadows are formed by ________ materials. (transparent/opaque)
4. The size of a shadow depends on the distance of the ________ from the light source. (object/shadow)
5. The colour of a shadow is always ________. (white/dark)

**D. Write two examples for each of the following.**

1. Transparent materials
2. Translucent materials
3. Opaque materials
4. Things required to form a shadow

**E. Give reasons for the following.**

1. Mirror is not a transparent object.
2. Transparent materials cannot form shadows.
3. A shadow does not show the details of the object except the outline of the shape of the object.
4. The shadow of an object formed by sunlight is the longest in the morning and evening.
5. Translucent objects form lighter shadows.

**F. Answer the following question briefly.**

1. What is the difference between transparent and translucent materials?
2. Why do transparent materials not form shadows?
3. State two factors on which the size of a shadow depends.

**G. Answer the following questions.**

1. Define transparent, translucent and opaque materials. Give two examples of each.
2. What is a shadow? What are the characteristics of a shadow?
3. Why is it that only translucent and opaque materials form shadows?

# Cognitive Corner

## Critical Thinking

1. You and your mother went to the market to buy new containers for her kitchen. What kind of containers would you suggest her to buy: opaque, transparent or translucent? Give reasons for your answer.
2. Isn't it because some refills and pens are transparent that you recognize the level of ink in them? Find out more devices which make use of transparent objects.

## Picture Study

Write transparent, translucent or opaque for each of the following:

1. 

Clear water

_______________

2. 

Bag

_______________

3. 

Frosted glass

_______________

4. 

Apple

_______________

## Project

Change a transparent object into translucent and opaque objects. Also, change an opaque object into a translucent object.

**Materials to be used:** A4 size transparent sheet of plastic, A4 size tracing paper (2 sheets), A4 size white opaque sheet (2 sheets), small bottle of hair oil, glue

**Procedure:**

1. Take a transparent plastic sheet. Stick tracing papers on both sides. (Apply glue only on the edges.) Now, the transparent plastic sheet becomes translucent. Paste one of the opaque white sheets on it. Can you see through it now?
2. Take an A4 size opaque white sheet. Rub two drops of coconut oil on the sheet and gently spread it. An oily patch will be formed on the sheet. Now, hold this sheet against a source of light (such as a bulb or a candle). Can you see the source of light through the patch?

## Life Skills

1. You are given the task of setting up your study room. Make a list of the materials you would need. Classify those materials as transparent, translucent and opaque. Justify their purpose and usage. Include two materials from each category.
2. Demonstrate the solar eclipse in the class using balls of different sizes and a source that emits parallel rays of light.

9 INDUSTRY, INNOVATION AND INFRASTRUCTURE

# Worksheet

The sun and stars are natural sources of light. On the Earth, we have learned to produce light from devices such as bulbs, LEDs and fluorescent tubes.

Electric bulbs

All these artificial sources of light operate on electricity.

We have also learned to harness the sun's light directly to produce electricity using solar panels. Solar panels are large panels containing a large number of solar cells that convert the sun's energy to electricity.

Solar street light

Sun's light is unlimited and free. It does not cause any pollution. So, the government is trying to use more solar energy. Solar street lights are installed in place of electric lights in many places.

Another great advantage of construction of solar panels for electricity is that these can be put up in remote places where it is difficult to lay down electric cables.

A. Mention two devices apart from solar panels that run on solar energy.

______________________________________________

______________________________________________

______________________________________________

B. Write some drawbacks of the devices that work on solar energy.

______________________________________________

______________________________________________

______________________________________________

# 13 Force and Energy

## Learning Checklist

- Effects of force
- Types of force
- Energy
- Simple machines

## Let's Get Started

Force and energy are the terms that we often use in our daily lives. To find out how much we know about force and energy, let us do this short exercise.

Look at the picture given below. Fill in the blanks using the correct options.

In a volleyball game, the ball hit by the players initially goes up, but always comes down due to ____________ (frictional/gravitational) force.

The referee on the side uses ____________ (sound/heat) energy from his whistle to control the game.

Since the game is mostly played indoors, the stadium needs to be sufficiently lit. The floodlights produce a lot of ____________ (light/sound) energy.

You have learned in Class 4 that **push** or **pull** are the two actions that make objects move, for example, a bullock pulling a cart, a man pushing a bike and a boy lifting his school bag.

**Force** is defined as a push or a pull applied on an object. Let us learn about the effects that force can produce.

## Effects of Force

### Force can make an object move

A force acting on a stationary object can make it move. Also, a force acting on a moving object can make it move faster, if the force is applied in the same direction in which the object is moving. For example, a football player kicks a ball to make it move, or a boy pushes a cart to make it move forward.

Force can move a cart

### Force can stop a moving object

A force acting on a moving object can slow it down or stop it completely, if it is applied in the direction opposite to the direction of motion.

For example, a goalkeeper uses his hands to stop a football from rolling into the net.

Force can stop a moving football

### Force can change the direction of a moving object

A force acting on a moving object from an angle can change the direction in which it is moving.

For example, in cricket, a batsman hits a moving ball with such force that it changes its direction.

Force can change the direction of a moving ball

### Force can change the shape of an object

A force acting on an object can change its shape.

Have you ever kneaded dough or made chapatis? Notice how a rolling pin makes a ball of dough flat and round when you apply force.

Another example is to squeeze a sponge and see how its shape changes.

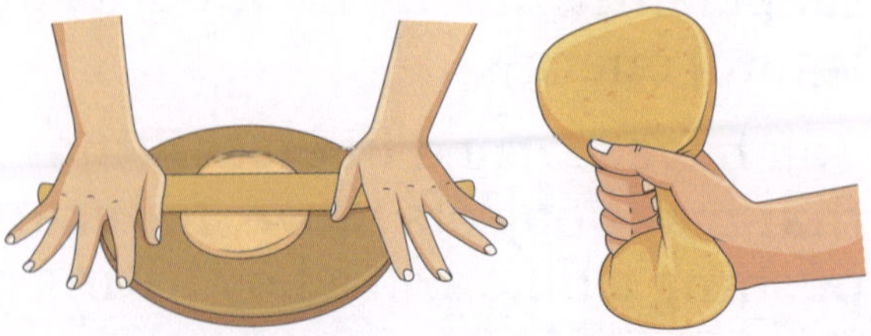

Force can change the shape of objects

# TYPES OF FORCE

Various types of forces exist in nature. Some of them are given below.

## Gravitational Force

**Gravitational force** is the force with which all objects in the universe attract each other. The gravitational force of the Earth, called gravity, pulls objects towards its centre. Any object that is thrown upwards always comes down because of the Earth's gravity. Gravitational force always acts in the opposite direction when an object moves away from the Earth; it acts along the direction of the motion of the object when it moves towards the Earth.

## Electrostatic Force

The attractive or repulsive force that acts due to the presence of 'charges' is called **electrostatic force**. Let us perform an activity to understand this better.

### Activity 1

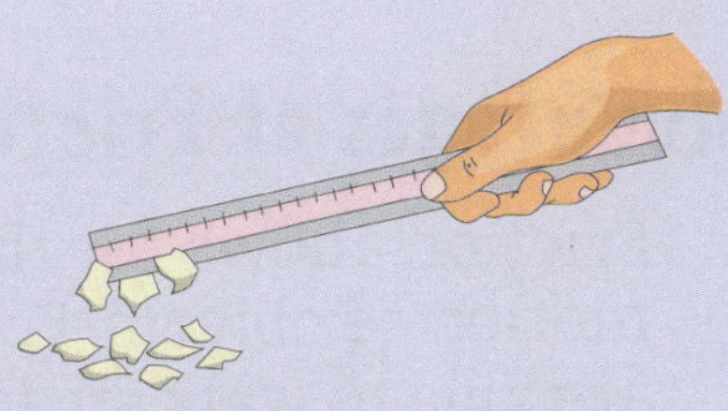

**Aim:** To understand electrostatic force

**Materials required:** Plastic ruler and bits of paper

**Procedure:**

1. Place bits of papers on a table.
2. Take the plastic ruler and rub it against your hair. Ensure that your hair is dry.
3. Bring the plastic ruler near the bits of paper and observe what happens.

**Observation:** You will find that the bits of paper move towards the plastic ruler.

**Conclusion:** The plastic ruler gets charged after being rubbed against your hair and the bits of paper get attracted towards it when it is brought closer.

You will learn more about electrostatic force in higher classes.

## Magnetic Force

**Magnets** are substances that attract certain materials towards them. The force with which a magnet attracts certain materials is called **magnetic force**.

Magnet attracts magnetic materials

Unlike poles attract and like poles repel

Magnetic force

The materials that get attracted towards a magnet are called **magnetic materials**. Materials that are made up of iron get attracted towards a magnet. That is, iron is a magnetic material.

Magnets also apply force on each other. Every magnet has two poles, known as the **north pole** and the **south pole**. When two poles of the same type are brought near each other, they repel or oppose each other, whereas, unlike poles attract each other.

## Frictional Force

**Frictional force** or **friction** acts on two objects that are in contact, and at least one of them is in motion. It always acts opposite to the direction of motion. Hence, it slows down the motion of an object or stops it from moving completely.

The force of friction produced depends on the nature of the objects in contact. Rough surfaces offer more friction than smooth surfaces. Let us learn about some of the advantages and disadvantages of friction.

### Advantages of Friction

- Friction allows for the steady motion of objects. For example, we are able to walk steadily due to the friction between the ground and our shoes. The grooves on the sole of our shoes provide enough friction to prevent us from falling. Vehicles move steadily on the road because of the friction between the tyres and the road.

Friction helps us to walk

- Friction produces heat, which we use for different purposes. For example, when a matchstick is struck against the rough surface of a matchbox, heat is produced due to friction, which lights the matchstick. When we rub our hands together, heat is produced due to friction that keep our hands warm.

A matchstick is rubbed a gainst a matchbox

## Disadvantages of Friction

- With increase in friction, it becomes difficult to move an object as more force is needed to overcome it. For example, moving heavy objects on a rough surface is difficult.
- Friction causes the surface of an object to wear out. For example, the soles of shoes and surface of tyres wear out because of friction.

# WORK

We are familiar with many activities in our daily life that involve work. What do we need to do work? We need to apply force to do work. When we apply force on an object, it moves in the direction in which the force is applied. If a force applied on an object moves it in the direction of the force, then work is said to be done.

The work done by a force depends on the amount of force applied and the distance through which the object is moved. If the amount of force applied is more, then the work done will also be more. Also, if the distance moved by the object is more, the work done will be more.

# ENERGY

The ability to do work is called **energy**. Energy is present around us in many forms, and we get it from different sources. For example, during the day, the sun gives out light and heat energy. At night, street lights use electrical energy to light the roads. The food we eat gives us the energy to work and play.

Let us now learn about the different forms of energy.

## Heat Energy

Heat energy

Heat is a form of energy. Heat energy is obtained from the sun, and also by burning fuels, such as coal, petrol and kerosene. We use heat energy for cooking food and to keep us warm.

## Light Energy

Light energy

Light energy helps us to see things around us. The sun is a natural source of light. Some artificial sources of light are electric bulb, candle, tubelight, lamp, etc. Plants also use light energy from the sun to prepare food.

## Mechanical Energy

A moving car has mechanical energy

The energy that an object has due to its position or its motion is called **mechanical energy**.

Mechanical energy is of two types: potential energy and kinetic energy. The energy that an object has due to its position with respect to the ground is called **potential energy**. For example, water stored in a dam or an overhead tank.

The energy that an object has due to its motion is called **kinetic energy**. All moving objects have kinetic energy. For example, a moving car and a bullet fired from a gun.

## Electrical Energy

Electrical energy

The most common and useful form of energy nowadays is electrical energy. This form can be easily converted to other forms of energy. Sources of electrical energy are cells and generators. Most of the common household appliances, such as fans, mobiles, watches, televisions and computers run on electrical energy.

## Sound Energy

Speaker

Sound is a form of energy that is produced by the vibration of objects. Some sources of sound energy include the radio, loudspeakers and musical instruments.

## Wind Energy

Windmill

The energy obtained from the moving wind is called wind energy. Windmills help in converting wind energy into electrical energy.

## Revise and Recall

**Fill in the blanks using the correct words.**

1. A stone thrown upwards falls down to the ground due to __________ acting on it. (magnetic force/gravitational force)
2. A football rolling on the ground comes to rest due to __________. (gravitational force/frictional force)
3. Materials made up of __________ are attracted by a magnet. (iron/aluminium)
4. The energy of an object due to its position is called __________. (potential energy/kinetic energy)
5. Loudspeaker is a source of __________ energy. (sound/electrical)

# SIMPLE MACHINES

Machines are tools that make our work easier by reducing the amount of force (effort) needed to do the work. Machines can be simple or complex.

Tools, such as scissors, screws, tongs and knives, that help us in doing work efficiently and easily, are called **simple machines**. There are six basic types of simple machines: lever, pulley, inclined plane, screw, wedge, and wheel and axle.

Complex machines are made of two or more simple machines. For example, a bicycle is a complex machine made up of lever, screw, and wheel and axle.

Let us learn more about simple machines.

## Lever

a

A lever is a rigid rod made to rest on and move around a fixed support. It consists of three parts:

**Fulcrum:** It is the fixed point or support on which the rod moves freely.

**Effort:** It is the force that is applied on the free end of the rod to enable the other end to perform work.

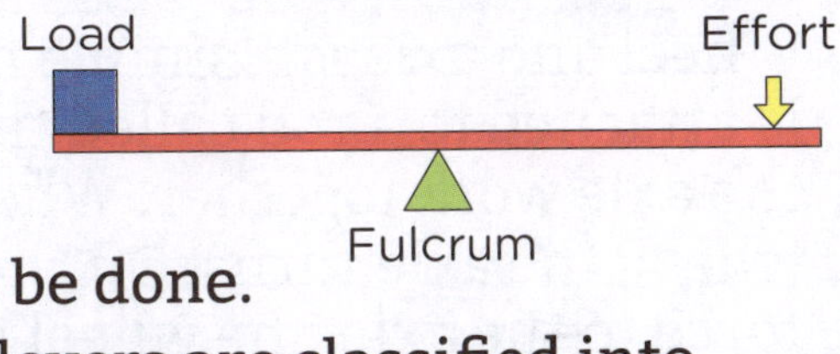


**Load:** It is the object on which work has to be done.

Depending on the position of these parts, levers are classified into three types: first-class, second-class and third-class.

**First-class levers:** In this type, the fulcrum is between the load and the effort. Some examples are scissors, crowbars, see-saw and claw hammers.

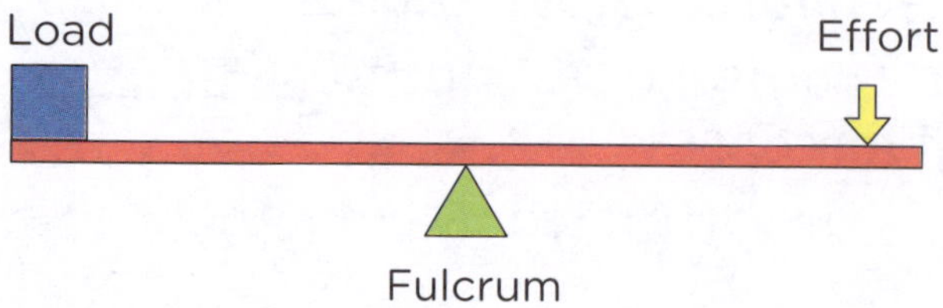


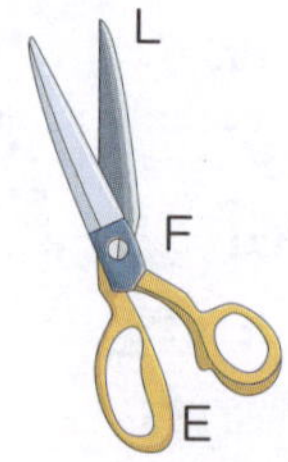

Scissors

See-saw

**Second-class levers:** Here, the load is between the effort and the fulcrum. Some examples are wheelbarrows, bottle openers and lemon squeezers.

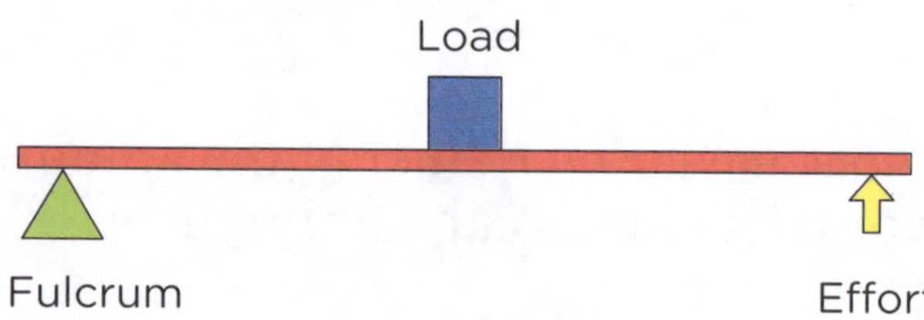


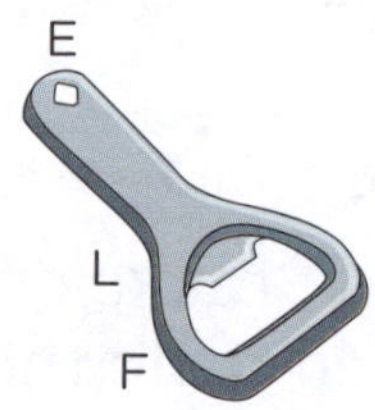

Bottle opener

Wheelbarrow

**Third-class levers:** In this type, the effort is between the fulcrum and the load. Some examples are a pair of tongs, a stapler, a fishing rod and tweezers.

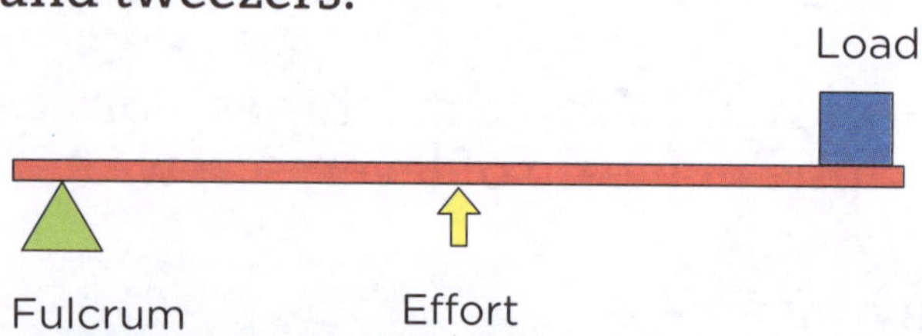


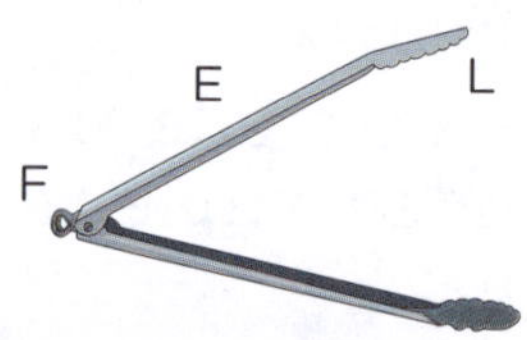

Tongs

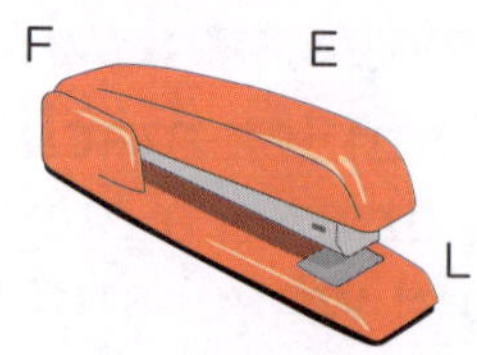

Stapler

**Science in Context**

When attempting to lift a load, the human hand acts as a third-class lever.

## Wheel and Axle

Wheel and axle is a simple machine in which a wheel is attached to a rod called the axle. The wheel and the axle work together. When force is applied to the wheel, the axle turns. On the other hand, if we apply force to the axle, the wheel turns. Some examples include steering wheels, door knobs and giant wheels.

Giant wheel

## Activity 2

**Aim:** To study the wheel and axle combination

**Materials required:** Four bottle caps, two pieces of thick broomstick (6 cm in length), two straws (4 cm in length), the matchstick holder of a matchbox and glue

**Procedure:**

1. Take the broomsticks and insert them into the straws.
2. Fix the bottle caps to the ends of the broomsticks to look like a wheel and axle.
3. Insert the broomsticks into the matchstick holder as shown in the image given alongside.
4. Place a weight on top of the matchstick holder and push the set-up from behind.

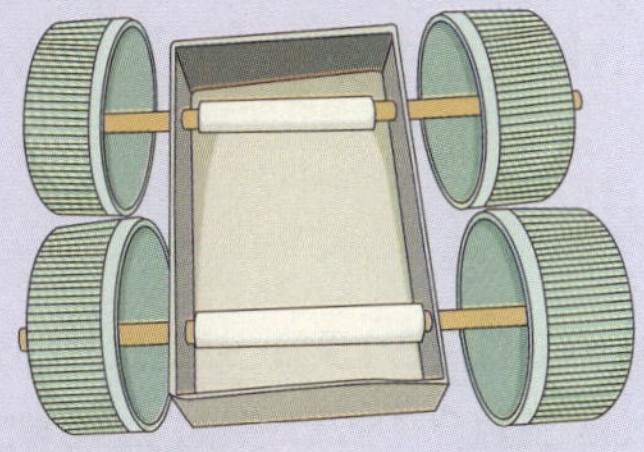

**Observation:** The set-up moves forward with the help of the wheel and the axle.

**Conclusion:** The wheel and axle combination makes work easier by reducing effort.

## Pulley

A pulley is made of a small wheel with a groove on its outer edge and a rope or chain running over the groove. The wheel rotates around an axle. They are used to lift weights. They are of two types: fixed and movable.

In a fixed pulley, the axle is attached to a support, such as a hook or the wall. It makes work easier by changing the direction of the force applied. Some examples are pulleys used in wells and on flagpoles.

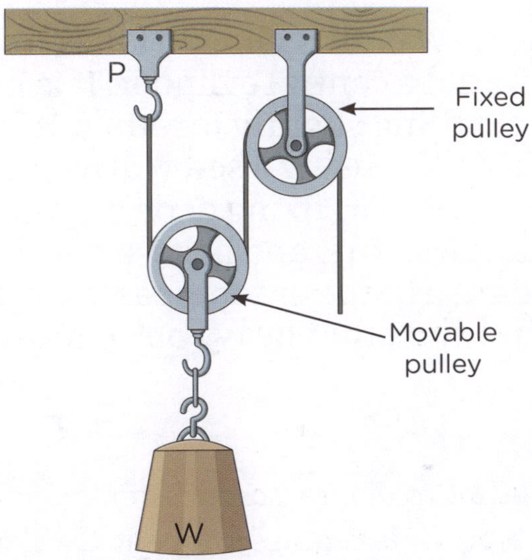

A pulley

A movable pulley is where the axle is not attached to any support and it is free to move along with the load. Movable pulleys are used, along with fixed pulleys, to reduce the effort. An example is cranes used in the construction sites to lift heavy loads with less effort.

## Inclined Plane

A slide

An inclined plane is a slope or a ramp or any slanting surface that helps to carry loads. It requires less force to move an object up an inclined plane than it does to lift the object vertically. Some examples are a slide in the park, ramps in hospitals to push wheelchairs up and down, and ramps for the loading and unloading goods on trucks and aeroplanes.

## Wedge

Knife

Axe

A wedge is a simple machine made by placing two surfaces, at least one of which is an inclined plane back to back, to form a sharp cutting surface. Some examples include the cutting edges of knives, needles and axes.

## Screw

Screw

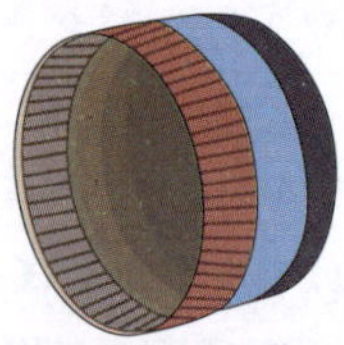

Bottle cap

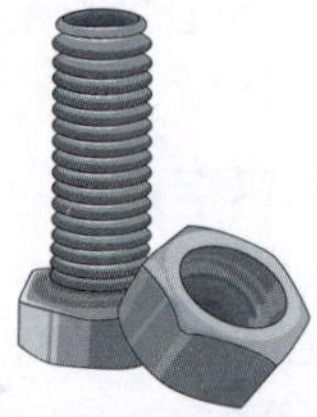

Nut and bolt

A screw is an inclined plane wrapped around a central cylinder. It is used to hold things tightly together. It can be turned by using a screwdriver. Screws are useful in fixing door hinges and handles. Nuts and bolts, a dentist's chair, a bottle or toothpaste cap and a screw jack (big screws used to lift cars and other heavy objects) are all examples of screws.

### Activity 3

**Aim:** To make a screw from an inclined plane

**Materials required:** A pencil, a sketch pen and a triangular sheet of paper

**Procedure:** Colour the inclined surface of the triangular paper. Now, wrap this paper around the pencil, so that the coloured surface faces outside.

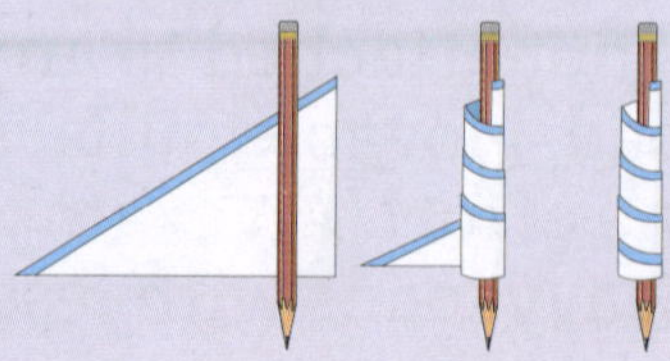

**Observation:** The coloured surface resembles a winding road or a staircase. We have, thus, made a screw out of an inclined plane.

## Keywords

**Magnetic force:** The force with which a magnet attracts certain materials

**Frictional force:** A force that acts on two objects that are in contact and at least one of them is in motion

**Heat energy:** Energy obtained by burning fuels such as oil and gas

**Mechanical energy:** Energy that an object has due to its position or motion

**Sound energy:** Energy produced by the vibration of objects

**Simple machine:** A tool or a device that makes work easier by reducing the effort

## Summary

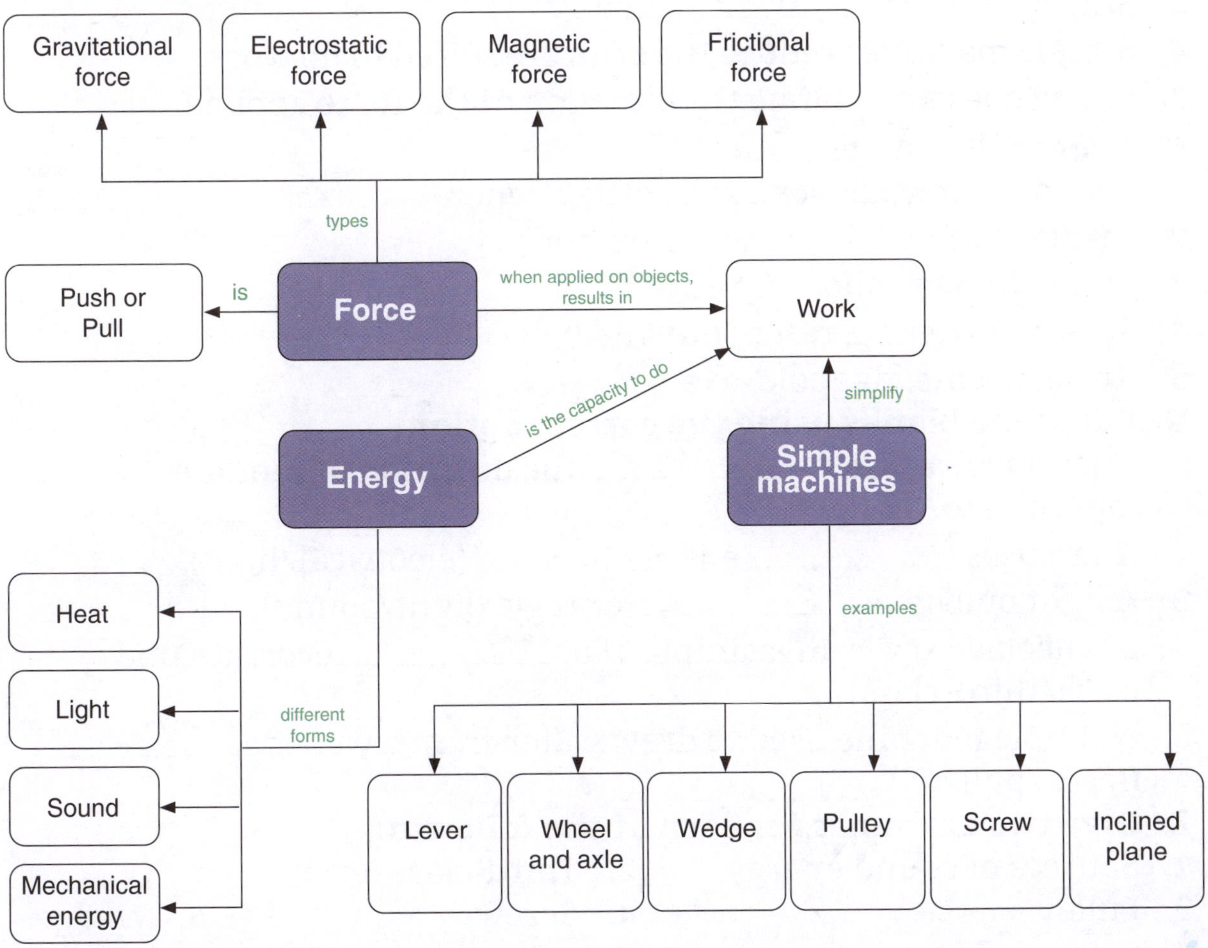

# Exercise

W

**A. Choose the correct option for each of the following.** ia

1. Which of the following is a type of force?
   (a) Electrostatic (b) Light (c) Sound (d) Heat
2. Which of the following is an example of a third-class lever?
   (a) Wheelbarrow (b) Tongs (c) See-saw (d) Bottle opener
3. Which of these forces is always attractive in nature?
   (a) Friction (b) Electrostatic
   (c) Gravity (d) Magnetic
4. Which of the following is not a simple machine?
   (a) Lever (b) Pulley (c) Bicycle (d) Wheel and axle

**B. State whether the following statements are true (T) or false (F).** ia

1. Force can change the direction of the motion of an object.
2. Energy and force are one and the same.
3. Sun is a source of only heat energy.
4. Simple machines reduce the effort required to do work.
5. Pulley does not change the direction of the force applied.

**C. Choose the odd one out.** ia

1. Scissors, crowbar, see-saw, bottle opener
2. Stapler, wheelbarrow, tweezers, tongs
3. Ramp, flyover, slide, see-saw
4. Screw, bottle cap, ramp, nut and bolt
5. Knife, needle, flagpole, axe

**D. Fill in the blanks using the correct option.**

1. Friction always acts ____________ the direction of motion. (opposite to/along)
2. A fan uses ____________ energy to work. (electrical/light)
3. A light bulb gives ____________ energy. (light/sound)
4. A wheelbarrow is an example of a ____________ lever. (second-class/third-class)
5. A simple machine used to draw water from a well is ____________ . (lever/pulley)

**E. Give two examples for each of the following.**

1. Sources of sound energy
2. Third-class lever
3. Pulley
4. Screw
5. Wedge

**F. Give reasons for the following.**

1. An object thrown upwards goes up and then falls down to the ground.
2. When a magnet is brought near an iron nail, it gets attracted to the magnet.
3. A matchstick rubbed on the match box catches fire.
4. A screw is used in door handles.
5. A ramp is used to shift heavy loads on to a truck.

**G. Answer the following questions briefly.**

1. Mention the effects of force on objects.
2. What is friction?
3. What is energy?
4. What is a simple machine?
5. What is fulcrum?

**H. Answer the following questions.**

1. Define friction. What are its advantages and disadvantages?
2. What is a lever? Explain the types of levers with one example of each.

## Cognitive Corner

### Critical Thinking

1. When you stand out in the sun, which energies would you be affected by?
2. How are nails different from screws? Which one will you use to hold things tightly?

### Picture Study

Identify the class of the levers shown in each of the images given below.

1. 
2. 
3. 

### Project

Identify the simple machines used in your house and make a list of them.

### Life Skills

Amit wants to unload some heavy luggages from a truck and carry them 20 metres to his house. Which simple machines can he use to make his task easier?

9 INDUSTRY, INNOVATION AND INFRASTRUCTURE

# Worksheet

The picture given alongside shows gears of different shapes and sizes. Gears are a very important part of the manufacturing world. Machines such as watches and vehicles need gears for working.

Gears of different sizes

If you look carefully, you will see that all these gears are circular in shape and have tooth-like structures, called **teeth of the gears**, surrounding them. The space between two teeth is kept the same for gears that work together. The teeth lock into each other. When one of these gears is rotated, the other gear locked into it also gets rotated.

In a watch, there are three main gears for its three hands.

The battery of the watch keeps the seconds gear in rotation. When this gear completes one rotation, it moves the minutes gear through one minute. Similarly, the minutes gear is joined to the hours gear. When the minutes gear completes one rotation, the hours gear moves through one hour.

Gears inside a watch

As the gears rotate, the hands displayed on the face of the watch rotate along with them, showing us the time.

A. Arrange the hands of a watch according to the time they take to complete one round, from the slowest to the fastest.

______________________________________________

B. Find out about another machine of daily use that uses gears for its working. Explain how that machine works. Paste the pictures of that machine in the box given below.

______________________________

______________________________

______________________________

______________________________

# 14 Measurement

**Learning Checklist**

- History of measurement
- Measurement of length, capacity, mass, time and temperature

## Let's Get Started

Finding out the size or quantity of something is called **measurement.** We measure many things in our day-to-day lives. Look at the pictures given below and complete the sentences.

① 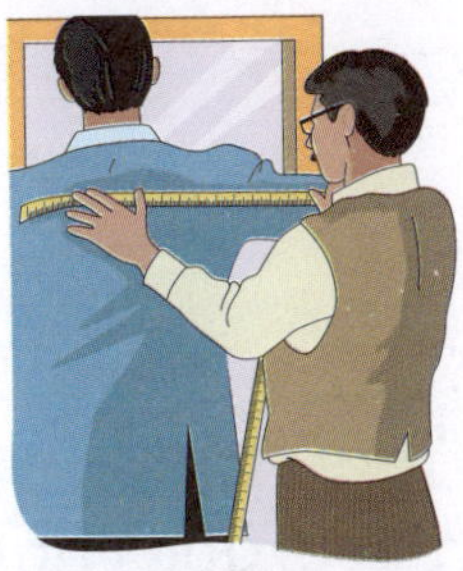

② 

③ 

④ 

1. The tailor is measuring the ______________ of the man's shoulder. (weight/length)
2. The greengrocer is ______________ the vegetables. (weighing/ carrying)
3. The milkman is measuring the ______________ of milk. (height/ quantity)
4. The doctor is measuring the ______________ of the patient. (weight/temperature)

Have you ever wondered how people in the ancient times used to measure things? What do you think were the methods used by them? Let us turn history and find out.

## HISTORY OF MEASUREMENT

In the earlier days, people used their body parts for measuring length.

Some of the body parts that was used to measure length were handspan, pace, cubit, foot and thumb.

### Activity 1

**Aim:** To check the reliability of the body parts for measurement

**Procedure:** Compare your handspan, cubit and foot size with that of your classmate and teacher, and find out if they are the same, smaller or bigger. Write your observation in the table given below.

**Observation:**

| Person | Handspan | Cubit | Foot |
|---|---|---|---|
| You | | | |
| Your friend | | | |
| Your teacher | | | |

**Conclusion:** The size of the body parts vary from person to person, and hence, the measurements taken using them will also vary.

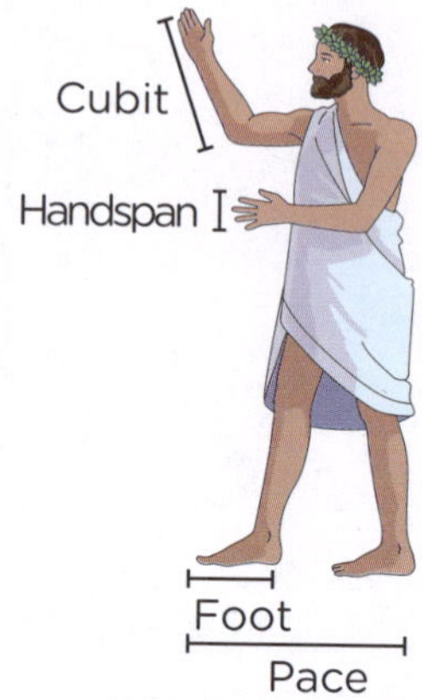


Body parts used for measurement in earlier days

From Activity 1, it is clear that the size of body parts differs from person to person. Hence, the measurement using body parts does not give accurate results. This has resulted in scientists to develop standard units for measurement, which would remain constant across the globe.

A fixed standard used for measurement is called **unit**. Length, mass, capacity, time and temperature are the different quantities we measure. We now have fixed units for the measurement of these quantities.

## MEASUREMENT OF LENGTH

a

Have you ever been to a shop to buy unstiched cloth material? The shopkeeper measures the cloth material with a long steel rod. It is a measuring rod that measures **length** in metres. The standard unit of the measurement of length is metre (m).

Smaller lengths, such as the length of your notebook, are measured in millimetre (mm) and centimetre (cm). Larger lengths, such as the distance between two cities, are measured in kilometre (km).

Relationship between different units for measuring length:

| | |
|---|---|
| 10 millimetres | = 1 centimetre |
| 100 centimetres | = 1 metre |
| 1000 metres | = 1 kilometre |

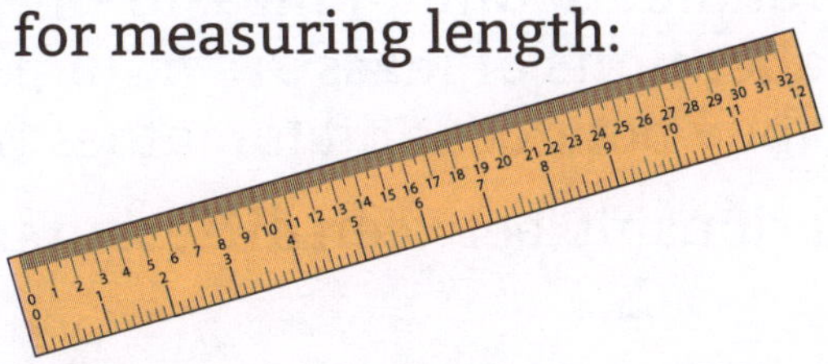

A ruler is used to measure small lengths

The common devices used to measure small lengths are a measuring tape and a ruler.

## MEASUREMENT OF CAPACITY

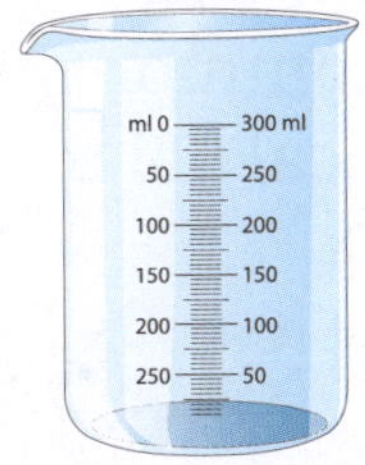


A beaker is used to measure the quantity of a liquid

The amount of liquid a container can hold is called the **capacity** of that container. The standard unit for the measuring capacity is litre (ℓ). We use millilitre (mℓ) for measuring smaller capacities and kilolitre (kℓ) for larger capacities. For example, a milkman gives milk in litres. At the hospital, a dropper is used to measure medicines in millilitres.

Relationship between the different units of measurement of capacity:

| | |
|---|---|
| 1000 millilitres | = 1 litre |
| 1000 litres | = 1 kilolitre |

Objects such as beakers and measuring cylinders are used to measure capacity.

### Revise and Recall

**Fill in the blanks using the correct words.**

1. People in ancient times measured the length of an object using __________. (ruler/handspan)
2. The standard unit of measurement of length is __________. (centimetre/metre)
3. 1 centimetre = __________. (100 metres/10 millimetres)
4. A milkman uses the unit __________ to measure milk. (kilogram/litre)
5. The amount of liquid a container can hold is the __________ of that container. (capacity/mass)

## MEASUREMENT OF MASS

The **mass** of a body or an object is the amount of matter present in it. The standard unit of measurement of mass is the kilogram (kg). The smaller units of mass are milligram (mg) and gram (g). For example, you buy potatoes and tomatoes from the greengrocer in kilograms.

Relationship between different units of measurement of mass:

| | |
|---|---|
| 1000 milligrams | = 1 gram |
| 1000 grams | = 1 kilogram |

A beam balance

The commonly used device for measuring mass is a physical balance (or beam balance).

## MEASUREMENT OF TIME

A particular moment in a day is called **time**. Time period is the duration between two events.

Measurement of time helps us to manage the activities in our daily lives effectively. For example, we know at what time we should wake up in the morning to be in time for school. When we know the timings of events and activities that are going to take place, we can manage our daily work accordingly.

A day is divided into 24 equal durations, and each duration is called an hour (h). Smaller durations are measured in minutes (min) and seconds (s), and larger durations are measured in weeks, months and years. The standard unit of measurement of time is a second.

Relationship between different units of measurement of time:

| | |
|---|---|
| 60 seconds | = 1 minute |
| 60 minutes | = 1 hour |
| 24 hours | = 1 day |
| 7 days | = 1 week |
| 12 months | = 1 year |

A wristwatch

A wall clock

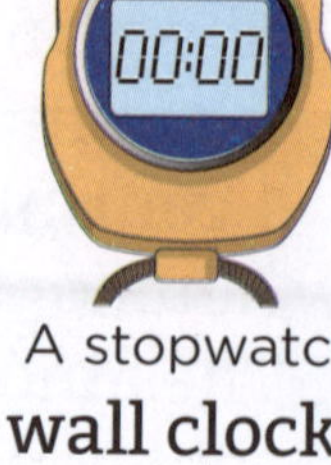


A stopwatch

The commonly used devices to measure time are watches, wall clocks and stopwatches.

### Science in Context

A year contains 365.25 days. It is difficult to represent 0.25 days every year. Therefore, it has been agreed globally to add one day to the month of February every fourth year, which is called a **leap year**. A leap year has 366 days, whereas a normal year has 365 days.

## MEASUREMENT OF TEMPERATURE

The degree of hotness or coldness of any object is called its **temperature**.

Temperature is commonly measured using the units degree Celsius (°C) and degree Fahrenheit (°F). The standard unit of measurement of temperature is kelvin (K).

Relationship between the different units of the measurement of temperature:

$$°C = \frac{5}{9}(°F - 32)$$

$$°F = \frac{9\ °C}{5} + 32$$

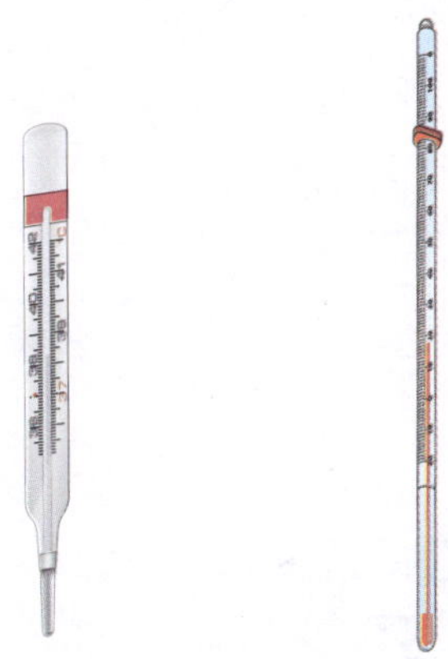

A clinical thermometer

A laboratory thermometer

The commonly used device for measuring temperature is a **thermometer**.

**Clinical thermometers** are used in hospitals for measuring body temperature. Has a doctor ever put a thermometer in your mouth and asked you to keep still for a minute or so? The doctor was actually checking you for fever. In other words, the doctor was checking how hot your body is. A **laboratory thermometer**, on the other hand, is used in a science laboratory for measuring the temperature of substances during experiments.

### Science in Context

Water boils at 100 °C.

Ice melts at 0 °C.

Normal temperature of the human body is 98.4 °F (37 °C).

## Keywords

**Measurement:** Finding out the size or the quantity of something
**Unit:** A fixed standard used for measurment
**Mass:** The amount of matter present in a body or an object
**Capacity:** The amount of liquid a container can hold
**Time:** A particular moment in a day
**Time period:** The duration between two events
**Temperature:** The degree of hotness or coldness of any object

## Summary

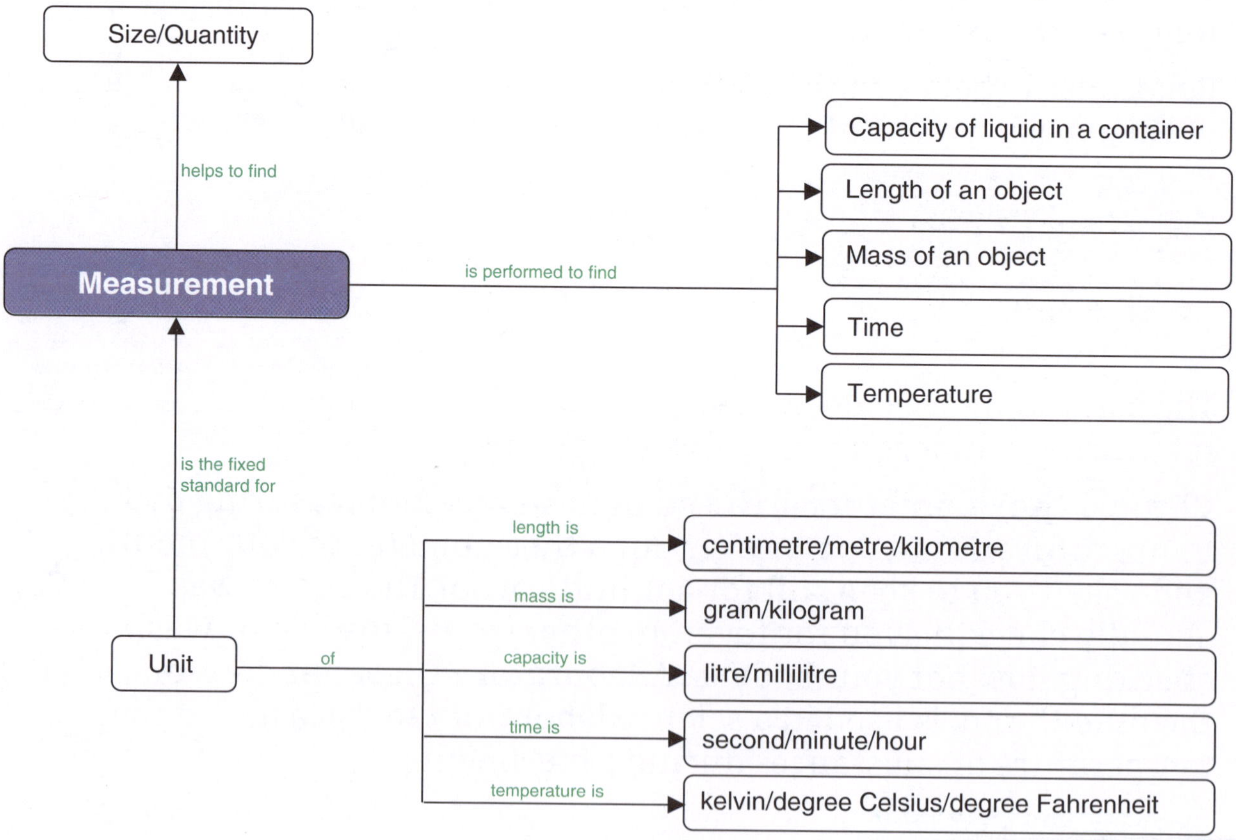

# Exercise

W

**A. Choose the correct option for each of the following.**

1. Identify the unit of length which is not related to a human body part.
   (a) Cubit (b) centimetre (c) Foot (d) Handspan
2. Which among the following is the biggest unit of length?
   (a) metre (b) millimetre (c) kilometre (d) centimetre
3. How many millilitres make one litre?
   (a) 1000 (b) 100 (c) 10 (d) 1
4. Which among the following is the smallest unit of time?
   (a) second (b) hour (c) minute (d) day

**B. Fill in the blanks using the correct option.** ia

1. Fixed standards used for measurement are called ____________. (cubit/units)
2. 1 kilometre is equal to ____________ metres. (100/1000)
3. The amount of matter present in an object is called its ____________. (mass/capacity)
4. 1 hour is equal to ____________ minutes. (24/60)

**C. State whether the following statements are true (T) or false (F).** ia

1. One centimetre is longer than one kilometre.
2. Litre is a unit of mass.
3. A day is divided into 24 equal durations.
4. Clinical thermometers are used by doctors.
5. Laboratory thermometers are used in a science laboratory.

**D. Name the following.** ia

1. The standard unit for the measurement of length
2. The standard unit for the measurement of capacity
3. The standard unit for the measurement of mass
4. The standard unit for measurement of time

**E. Give reasons for the following.**

1. Measurement using body parts is not accurate.
2. We do not use measuring tapes and rulers to measure the distance between two cities.
3. Generally, we express the length of our text book in centimetres.
4. The units of temperature degree Celsius and degree Fahrenheit are not same.
5. A clinical thermometer is different form a laboratory thermometer.

**F. Answer the following questions briefly.**

1. What is measurement?
2. What is capacity?
3. Define time and time period.
4. What is the relationship between degree Celsius and degree Fahrenheit?

**G. Answer the following questions.**

1. Name three body parts used in the earlier days for measuring length. What is the drawback of using these body parts for measuring length?
2. What are the five different quantities of measurement? Also, mention the standard units and devices used for measuring them.
3. Define temperature. Name the various units used to measure temperature. What is the device used for measuring temperature?

# Cognitive Corner

## Critical Thinking

Normal school timing is approximately 7 hours a day. Express it in terms of minutes.

## Picture Study

Write the quantities measured using the devices given below.

1 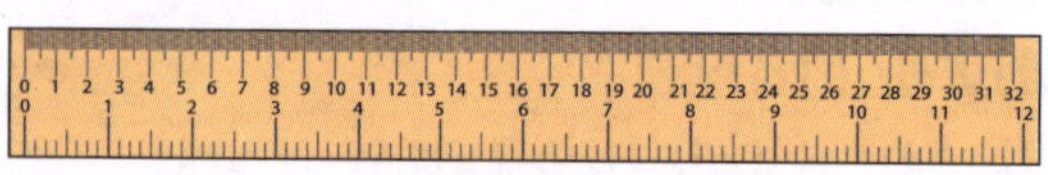


__________

2. 

__________

## Project

Measure the length of the teacher's table in your classroom by using your handspan and then using a scale. Record your readings in a notebook. Compare your readings with that of your classmates' and find out in which of the cases you got a uniform reading of measurement.

## Life Skills

Amanthi has a fever and her mother wanted to check her body temperature. She pulled out a laboratory thermometer from her father's cupboard and tried to measure Amanthi's temperature. Even after multiple attempts, she was not able to get the correct temperature. Why?

# Worksheet

Thermometers are instruments that are used to measure temperature. Some thermometers use a liquid called mercury inside the tubes. There is also another kind of thermometer which uses alcohol instead of mercury.

Mercury thermometer

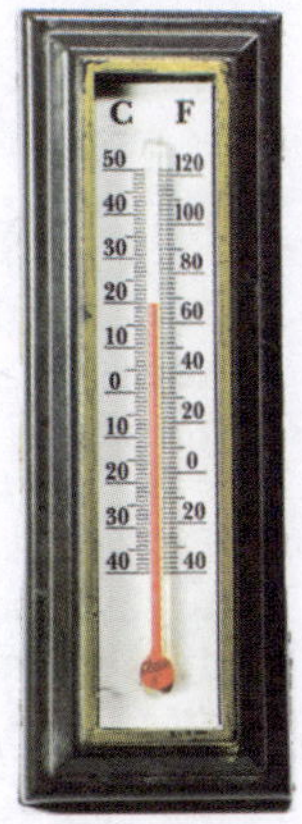

Alcohol thermometer

A. Mercury thermometers can be used to measure temperatures between –37 °C and 356 °C. Alcohol thermometers can be used to measure temperatures between –112 °C and 78 °C.

1. Which thermometer will be suitable in very cold climates? Why?

   ______________________________

2. Which thermometer will be suitable to measure high temperatures?

   ______________________________

3. Mercury thermometers are no longer in use nowadays. Find out the reason why. Name an alternative thermometer that can be used instead of a mercury thermometer.

   ______________________________

B. Do a research on other types of thermometers. Collect pictures of as many thermometers as you can and paste them in the space provided below. If possible, write one advantage and one disadvantage of each thermometer.

# Vernacular Names

**Seal** • Assamese: *Samudri prani* • Hindi: *Seel* • Kannada: *Neeru naie* • Malayalam: *Kaṭalnāy* • Marathi: *Himācchādita ṭuṇḍrā pradēśātīla jalacara prāṇī* • Tamil: *Kadal nai* • Telugu: *Ubhayacaramu* • Urdu: *Deriyai bajara*

**Walrus**• Assamese: *Jl-ghottk* • Bengali: *Sindhughotok* • Hindi: *Vaalaras* • Kannada: *Kadala simha* • Malayalam: *vālṟas* • Marathi: *Vŏlarasa* • Tamil: *Kaṭaṟkutirai* • Telugu: *Vālras* • Urdu: *Barkhani sher*

**Sea horse** • Assamese: *Samundari akshohin* • Hindi: *Samudree ghoda* • Kannada: *Samudra kudure, Meenashwa* • Marathi: *Samudrī ghōḍā* • Malayalam: *Kaṭal kutira* • Tamil: *Kaṭaṟkutirai* • Telugu: *Samudra gurraṁ* • Urdu: *Samundari ghoda*

**Sea turtle** • Assamese: *Samundari siisrp* • Bengali: *Shamudrik Kachhap* • Hindi: *Samudree kachhua* • Kannada: *Samudra āme* • Meiteilon: *Theng-gu* • Marathi: *Samudrī kāsava* • Malayalam: *Kaṭalāma* • Mizo: *Sumsi* • Tamil: *Kaṭal āmai* • Telugu: *Samudra tābēlu* • Urdu: *Samundari kachuva*

**Jellyfish** • Assamese: *Jeli-maacha* • Hindi: *Jelifish* • Kannada: *Jelli mīnu* • Marathi: *Jēlī phiśa* • Malayalam: *jelliphiṣ* • Tamil: Illlutu miinnn • Telugu: *Jellīphiṣ*

**Crane** • Assamese: *Kren* • Bengali: *Sharosh* • Hindi: *Saaras* • Kannada: *Kokkare* • Meiteilon: *U-rok* • Marathi: *Krēna pakṣī* • Malayalam: *Kreyin pakṣi* • Mizo: *Kanghlai* • Tamil: *Kokku* • Telugu: *Krēn pakṣi* • Urdu: *Saris*

**Snail** • Assamese: *Ambu* • Bengali: *Shamuk* • Hindi: *Ghongha* • Kannada: *Basavana hula* • Meiteilon: *Tharoi* • Marathi: *Gōgalagāyī kiḍā* • Malayalam: *Occa* • Mizo: *Hawngkawrawi* • Tamil: *Nattai* • Telugu: *Natta* • Urdu: *Gondha*

**Cockroach** • Assamese: *Tilachatta* • Bengali: *Tēlāpōkā* • Hindi: *Tilachatta* • Kannada: *Jirale* • Meiteilon: *Kharmi* • Marathi: *Jhuraḷa* • Malayalam: *Pāṟṟa* • Mizo: *Khau-hriang* • Tamil: *Karappāṉ Poochi* • Telugu: *Boddiṅka* • Urdu: *Till Chitta*

**Maple** • Assamese: *Maple* • Bengali: *Kirmoli, Br̥kṣabiśēṣa* • Hindi: *Pharjanj* • Kannada: *Buzim-pala* • Marathi: *Mĕpala* • Malayalam: *Mēppiḷ* • Mizo: *Thing-phing-phi-hlip* • Tamil: *Mēppiḷ* • Telugu: *Māpul* • Urdu: *Tarkanna*

**Mistletoe** • Assamese: *Amer bel* • Bengali: *Dhaira, Banda* • Hindi: *Budu, Pudu, Hurchu* • Kannada: *Badanike* • Marathi: *Banda* • Malayalam: *ittikkanni* • Mizo: *Lenpat* • Tamil: *pulluruvi* • Telugu: *Mundla kampa, Puttu, Tella uppi* • Urdu: *Amar bail*

**Onion** • Assamese: *Aamlett* • Bengali: *Pneyaj* • Hindi: *Pyaaj* • Kannada: *Īruḷḷi, ullagaddi* • Meiteilon: Tilhou • Marathi: *Kāndā* • Malayalam: *uḷḷi*• Mizo: *Purun* • Tamil: *Veṅkāyam* • Telugu: *Ullipāya* • Urdu: *Pyaz*

***Bryophyllum*** • Assamese: *Paategjaa* • Bengali: *Pathorkuchi* • Hindi: *Paanphuttii* • Kannada: Brayōphilam • Meiteilon: *Manahidak* • Marathi: *Brāyōphilama* • Malayalam: *Brayēāphillaṁ* • Mizo: *Hnahchhah* • Tamil: *Piraiyōpillam* • Telugu: *Bryophyllum* • Urdu: *Zakhmhaiyat*

---

What do you call these plants and animals in your language? Share the names with us at **schoolsupport@harpercollins.co.in.**

Collins

Adheres to National Education Policy
PREPARATORY STAGE

# SUPPLEMENTARY BOOKLET

# 5

## Enhanced Science Now

Series Editor | Jyothsna Natraj

# About the STEAM Activities

In the 21st century where the world is rapidly changing with sudden disruptions and unexpected real-world problems, being skilled in just one stream may not be enough. Many real-world problems can be solved only through interdisciplinary approach. Moreover, educationists have been emphasizing on the importance of subject integration and cross-curricular links. **Science**, **technology**, **engineering**, **arts** and **maths** (**STEAM**) education is one such approach where the integration of these five disciplines is utilized to solve real-world problems. Through this approach, a variety of skills such as critical thinking, creativity, innovation, communication, collaboration and entrepreneurship can be applied to make the students ready for the future, where these skills would be applicable in any field of study.

Students need to be introduced to STEAM education early on in life while their mind is still full of curiosity and imagination. STEAM education would not only help in producing tomorrow's designers and engineers, it would also help develop innovative mindsets and the ability to solve real-world problems. This would bring the students one step closer to becoming innovators or creators, not just passive consumers.

This supplementary booklet which comes along with ***Enhanced Science Now*** series, aims to introduce STEAM education to students from classes 1 to 8. There are two problems, based on ***real-world contexts***, in each booklet. The contexts have been carefully designed and mapped directly with the syllabus of each class. The students would be applying interdisciplinary concepts they have learnt in a class to find solution to the given problems. With each problem, research tips have been given to help in the initiation of idea. Clear directives have been given for students to identify the problem, research and record data, record their thinking, sketch their ideas, make observations and improve their design or solution as they work through creating the design or solving the problem.

We hope the students, while applying the concepts they have learnt to solve the real-world problems, would find their learning meaningful and thus be inspired to become future problem solvers, critical thinkers, innovators or inventors.

Content Developed by Excelsoft Technologies Pvt Ltd.

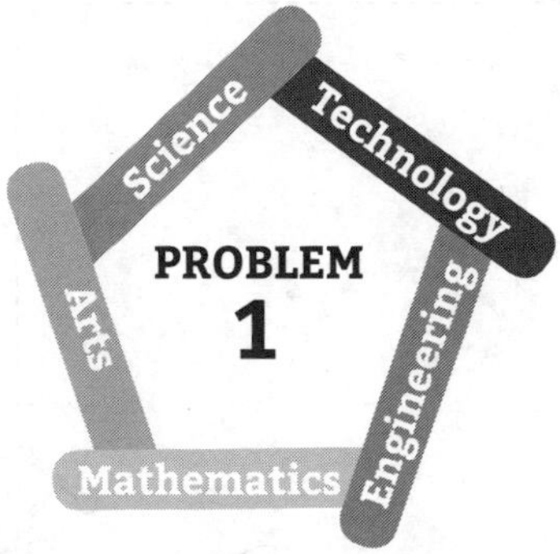


Amit was watching the construction of a building. He saw a construction worker carrying the materials to the top of the building using a wooden ladder. He noticed that it is too laborious, time consuming and risky.

He decided to design a device/equipment to minimize the effort and hence lift heavy objects to a height easily. Help Amit in understanding about the devices used to make the work easier by minimizing the efforts. Then, help him design a prototype of a device for lifting heavy objects to a height easily.

**Statement of the problem:**

______________________________________________

______________________________________________

______________________________________________

______________________________________________

______________________________________________

**Research tips:**

1. Simple machines
2. Pulleys, fixed pulleys and movable pulleys
3. Combination of pulleys to reduce the effort.

**Gather information relevant for this problem.**

1. ______________________________________________
   ______________________________________________
2. ______________________________________________
   ______________________________________________
3. ______________________________________________
   ______________________________________________
4. ______________________________________________
   ______________________________________________

**Draw/sketch your design.**

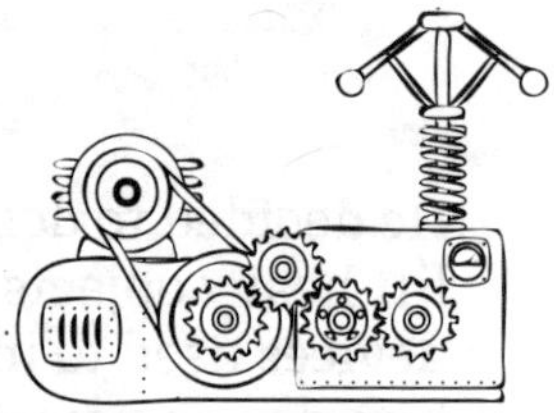

**Materials required:**

______________________________

______________________________

______________________________

______________________________

______________________________

**Construction (Write down the steps to construct your design):**

1. ______________________________

   ______________________________

2. ______________________________

   ______________________________

3. ______________________________

   ______________________________

4. ______________________________

   ______________________________

**Implementation of the prototype (try out your model):**

Step 1: ____________________

Step 2: ____________________

Step 3: ____________________

Step 4: ____________________

**Observation (What worked? What did not work?):**

____________________

____________________

____________________

____________________

____________________

**Scope for improvement (How can you make it better?):**

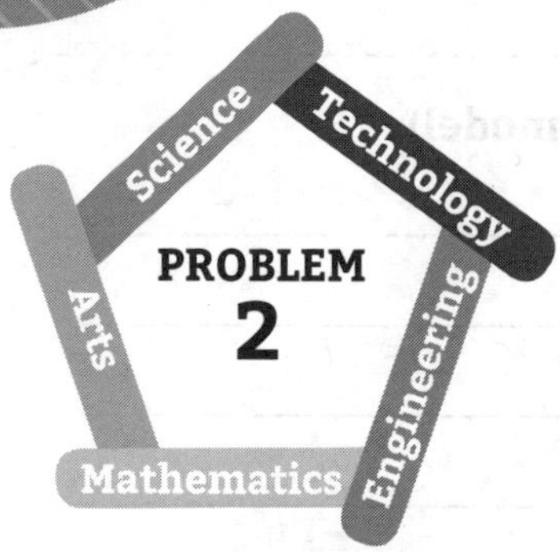


John wants to study about the properties of shadows formed by objects with different shapes and colours. He also wants to know about the image of these objects formed by a plane mirror.

He decided to design an experiment to study the shadows formed by different objects with different shape and colours. Also, he wanted to compare the shadows in each case with an image of the same object in a mirror.

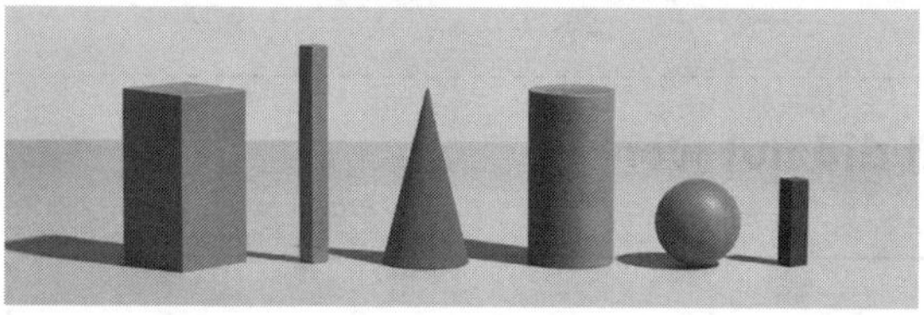

Help John device a set-up to conduct the experiment and hence to achieve the results.

**Statement of the problem:**

______________________________

______________________________

______________________________

______________________________

______________________________

**Research tips:**

1. Shadows
2. Images
3. Image formed by a plane mirror

**Gather information relevant for this problem.**

1. ______________________________

   ______________________________

2. ______________________________

   ______________________________

3. ______________________________

   ______________________________

4. ______________________________

   ______________________________

**Draw/sketch your design.**

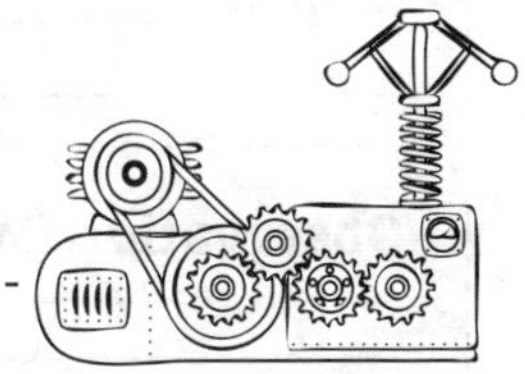

**Materials required:**

______________________________

______________________________

______________________________

______________________________

______________________________

**Construction (Write down the steps to construct your design):**

1. ______________________________

______________________________

2. ______________________________

______________________________

3. ______________________________

______________________________

4. ______________________________

______________________________

**Implementation of the prototype (try out your model):**

Step 1: ______________________________

Step 2: ______________________________

Step 3: ______________________________

Step 4: ______________________________

**Observation (What worked? What did not work?):**

______________________________

______________________________

______________________________

______________________________

______________________________

**Scope for improvement (How can you make it better?):**

**STEAM Vocabulary**

**Construction:** The way in which a thing is built or put together

**Implementation:** Trying out/carrying out/experimenting

**Prototype:** A working model of a new product/new version of an old product

**Scope:** Possibility

# Assessment 1

**CHAPTERS 1–4**

(Maximum Marks = 25)

**A. Choose the correct option for each of the following.** **(7 × 1 = 7)**

1. Embryo, cotyledon and hilum are found in
   (a) Fruit (b) Seed (c) Flower (d) Stem
2. Which of the following is a common feature in dandelion, maple and cotton plants?
   (a) They grow to the same height
   (b) They have the same leaf colour
   (c) They have round and spiky seeds
   (d) They have hairy and wing-shaped seeds
3. Which of the following has scales as its body covering?
   (a) Snail (b) Snake (c) Sheep (d) Swan
4. Which of the following animal breathes with the help of gills?
   (a) Earthworm (b) Cockroach (c) Dolphin (d) Prawn
5. Which of the following has a hinge joint?
   (a) Knee (b) Shoulder (c) Wrist (d) Foot
6. The other name of the bony box that protects the brain is
   (a) Cranium (b) Cervix (c) Rib (d) Spine
7. Which of the following helps in the growth and repair of tissues?
   (a) Carbohydrates (b) Proteins (c) Vitamins (d) Fats

**B. State whether the following statements are true (T) or false (F).** **(6 × 1 = 6)**

1. Cotyledon is the source of food for the developing baby plant. ☐
2. Berries are dispersed by the wind. ☐
3. Fishes swim with the help of their webbed feet. ☐
4. Desert habitats are dry and sandy lands with scanty rainfall. ☐
5. The hinge joint is located between the skull and the backbone. ☐
6. Vegetables and fruits are good sources of roughage. ☐

**C. Replace the underlined word in each of the following sentences with the correct word.** **(6 × 1 = 6)**

1. <u>Reproduction</u> is the process by which a plant grows from a seed.
2. A plant with a hook-like structure on its seeds is <u>sandspur</u>.
3. <u>Lungs</u> are the breathing organs of insects.

4. Pivot joint is present in the elbows, knees, fingers and toes.
5. Anaemia is caused due to the deficiency of vitamin A.
6. A diet containing the right proportions of various nutrients is known as the chemical diet.

**D. Name the following.** **(6 × 1 = 6)**

1. The structure that protects the cotyledons and the baby plant inside a seed
2. The largest habitat of the world
3. The tough elastic tissue that is present in the ear and the nose
4. The muscles that are under our control
5. The process of using vaccines for the prevention of diseases
6. The state of complete physical and mental well-being

# Assessment 2

**CHAPTERS 5–7**

(Maximum Marks = 25)

**A. Pick the odd one out from each of the following groups of words.** **(7 × 1 = 7)**

| | | | | |
|---|---|---|---|---|
| 1. | Sprain | Snake bite | Fracture | Sling |
| 2. | Fracture | Bee sting | Rabies | Snake bite |
| 3. | Troposphere | Biosphere | Mesosphere | Stratosphere |
| 4. | Sedimentation | Distillation | Evaporation | Chlorination |
| 5. | Ozone | Oxygen | Nitrogen | Meteors |
| 6. | Earth | Venus | Mars | Moon |
| 7. | Mantle | Core | Corona | Crust |

**B. Circle YES if the statement is correct and NO if it is wrong.** **(6 × 1 = 6)**

1. Ganesh fractured his leg. Should he run around and play for the quick healing of the fracture? Yes No
2. Should we tie a tight elastic bandage just above the blisters formed due to burns? Yes No
3. Is it a good practice to give first aid before taking a patient to the hospital? Yes No
4. Distilled water is the purest form of water. Yes No
5. The Earth's atmosphere protects us from the harmful radiations of the sun. Yes No
6. Moon has a thick atmosphere around it. Yes No

**C. Fill in the blanks using the correct words.** **(6 × 1 = 6)**

1. A person who has been injured or attacked is called a ________________ . (culprit/victim)
2. A strap or cloth that goes under the arm and then around the neck to support the fractured arm is called ________________. (sling/scarf)
3. In water purification, alum is added during the process of ________________ . (sedimentation/distillation)
4. ________________ gas is released during photosynthesis. (Oxygen/Carbon dioxide)
5. The innermost layer of the Earth is known as ________________ . (core/mantle)
6. The surface temperature of sun is about ________________ degree Celsius. (600/6000)

**D. Name the following.** **(6 × 1 = 6)**

1. The device used to put out a fire
2. The amount of water present in the air
3. The chemical used to increase the rate of sedimentation
4. The eclipse that occurs when the moon comes between the sun and the Earth
5. The layer from which magma comes out to the surface of the Earth during volcanic eruptions
6. An object moving around a planet in the solar system

# Assessment 3

**CHAPTERS 8–11**

(Maximum Marks = 25)

**A. Choose the correct option for each of the following.** **(7 × 1 = 7)**

1. Global warming is caused due to the increase in the level of
   (a) Oxygen (b) Water (c) Carbon dioxide (d) Dust
2. Which of the following is a major cause of soil erosion?
   (a) Oil spill (b) Vehicles (c) Global warming (d) Deforestation
3. Hot magma reaching the Earth's surface is called
   (a) Vent (b) Lava (c) Volcano (d) Focus
4. Which of the following is not an after-effect of floods?
   (a) Loss of life (b) Damage to property
   (c) Change in weather pattern (d) Spread of disease

5. Which among the following is an igneous rock?
   (a) Obsidian (b) Sandstone (c) Limestone (d) Slate
6. The rock that contained pebbles and boulders held together by minerals is called
   (a) Conglomerate (b) Sandstone (c) Pumice (d) Slate
7. The formation of mist is an example of
   (a) Freezing (b) Melting (c) Evaporation (d) Condensation

**B. State whether the following statements are true (T) or false (F).** **(6 × 1 = 6)**

1. Global warming melts the ice in polar regions.
2. Asthma is caused due to water pollution.
3. Tides reach the maximum height when both the sun and the Earth are in line with each other.
4. A vent is a region where the Earth's crust is weak and develops a crack.
5. Marble and slate are examples of metamorphic rocks.
6. All solids contract on cooling.

**C. Replace the underlined word in each of the following sentences with the correct word.** **(6 × 1 = 6)**

1. <u>Noise</u> pollution is a major cause of diarrhoea.
2. Soil erosion can be prevented by <u>deforestation</u>.
3. Intensity of an earthquake is determined by using an instrument called <u>barometer</u>.
4. <u>Marble</u> is formed due to the slow cooling of magma.
5. <u>Oxygen</u> is the major constituent of air.
6. Ozone layer is found in the region of the atmosphere called <u>exosphere</u>.

**D. Answer each of the following questions in one word.** **(6 × 1 = 6)**

1. The removal of topsoil by wind and water.
2. The types of volcanoes that have not erupted for a long period, but have the potential to lead to a possible eruption.
3. The rock that is also called volcanic glass.
4. The non-metallic mineral commonly used in thermal power generation.
5. The gas used during the process of photosynthesis.
6. The chemical used to kill germs during water purification.

# Assessment 4

**CHAPTERS 12-14**
(Maximum Marks = 25)

**A. Pick the odd one out from each of the following groups of words. (7 × 1 = 7)**

| | | | | |
|---|---|---|---|---|
| 1. | Butter paper | Plain glass | Tracing paper | Frosted glass |
| 2. | Leather jacket | Silver plate | Butter paper | Leaf |
| 3. | Plain water | Plain glass | Frosted glass | Plain plastic |
| 4. | Bulb | Candle | Torch | Guitar |
| 5. | Handspan | Cubit | Foot | Metre |
| 6. | Scissors | Bottle opener | Knife | Tongs |
| 7. | Scale | Inch tape | Beam balance | Human foot |

**B. Circle YES if the following statement is correct and NO if it is wrong. (6 × 1 = 6)**

1. All opaque objects form shadow. Yes No
2. All transparent objects form shadow. Yes No
3. Force can set a stationary object into motion. Yes No
4. Gravitational force is a repulsive force. Yes No
5. One hour is equal to 3600 seconds. Yes No
6. Measuring jar is a measuring device for mass. Yes No

**C. Fill in the blanks with the correct words. (6 × 1 = 6)**

1. Shadows are always ____________ in colour. (dark/white)
2. Spectacles are made of ____________ material. (transparent/ translucent)
3. The ____________ force is both attractive and repulsive in nature. (magnetic/gravitational)
4. A ____________ surface will offer more friction. (smooth/rough)
5. A day is divided into ____________ hours. (24/30)
6. The SI unit of the measurement of temperature is ____________ . (degree Celsius/kelvin)

**D. Answer each of the following questions in one word. (6 × 1 = 6)**

1. The materials that allow light to pass through them partially
2. The force that comes into play when the surfaces of two objects are in contact with each other
3. The energy produced by vibrating bodies
4. The device used for measuring temperature
5. A unit for measuring mass other than kilogram
6. One litre expressed in millilitre

# Comprehensive Assessment 1

**CHAPTERS 1-7**

(Maximum Marks = 50)

**A. Name the following.** **(10 × 1 = 10)**

1. The reproductive structures in ferns.
2. The natural surroundings where living organisms live.
3. The structures that attach muscles to bones.
4. The type of the joint present in elbows, knees, fingers and toes.
5. The type of disease that is passed from an infected person to a healthy person.
6. The immediate treatment given to an injured person before taking him/her to a hospital.
7. The process through which the oxygen content of water is increased.
8. The layer where most meteors burn up while entering the Earth's surface.
9. The process in which a pure liquid is separated from a mixture of liquids.
10. The outer layer of the sun.

**B. In each of the following questions, two choices are correct. Identify the correct choices.** **(9 × 2 = 18)**

1. A rose plant can be grown from
   (a) Stem cutting (b) Root (c) Tendril
   (d) Seed (e) Leaf (f) Grafting
2. Identify the animals that belong to a polar habitat.
   (a) Walrus (b) Camel (c) Whale
   (d) Penguin (e) Fish (f) Deer
3. Which joint allows movement in all directions?
   (a) Hinge and pivot joint (b) Ball and socket joint
   (c) Hip joint and shoulder joint (d) Wrist and ankle joint
   (e) Backbone and head joint (f) Ankle and hinge joint
4. Identify the deficiency disorders from the following.
   (a) Flu (b) Anaemia (c) Chicken pox
   (e) Scurvy (d) Cholera (f) Measles
5. Assume that your friend has sprained his/her ankle. Which of the following would you do?
   (a) Keep his/her ankle on a chair and tilt the position of the ankle.
   (b) Ask him/her not to move the sprained part.

(c) Ask him/her to get up and run in order to avoid stiffness.
(d) Wrap an elastic bandage around the sprained area.
(e) Massage the sprained area with any massage cream and apply heat over it.
(f) Apply pressure over the sprained area and put some ice packs over it.

6. Identify the uses of oxygen.
   (a) Preparing fertilizers
   (b) Required for respiration
   (c) Increases soil fertility
   (d) Used during photosynthesis
   (e) Required for burning
   (f) For pollination

7. What are the characteristic features of air?
   (a) Exerts pressure
   (b) Does not occupy space
   (c) Weightless
   (d) Mixture of gases
   (e) Pure substance
   (f) Liquid state

8. Which of the following statements are true for a lunar eclipse?
   (a) The moon is covered by the shadow of the Earth.
   (b) The Earth is covered by the shadow of the moon.
   (c) The sun is covered by the shadow of the moon.
   (d) The Earth comes between the sun and the moon.
   (e) The moon comes between the sun and the Earth.
   (f) The sun comes between the Earth and the moon.

9. Which of the following are the layers of the Earth?
   (a) Corona
   (b) Mantle
   (c) Troposphere
   (d) Ionosphere
   (e) Crust
   (f) Ozone layer

**C. Answer the following questions.** **(2 × 3 = 6)**

1. What are three types of nerves in the human body?
2. What is solar system? Name the different members of the solar system.

**D. Answer the following questions in detail.** **(4 × 4 = 16)**

1. Briefly explain the processes involved in agriculture.
2. Briefly explain the various types of habitats with their examples.
3. List the symptoms and preventive measures of the following deficiency disorders.
   (a) Beri-beri
   (b) Goitre
4. How will you give first aid to someone bitten by a stray dog?

# Comprehensive Assessment 2

**CHAPTERS 8–14**

(Maximum Marks = 50)

**A. Name the following.** **(10 × 1 = 10)**

1. The term used for substances that cause pollution
2. The outermost layer of the Earth
3. The region where the Earth's crust tends to be weak and develops a crack
4. One example of a sedimentary rock
5. The main constituent of the rock limestone
6. The tiny particles that matter is made up of
7. The category of materials to which an egg belongs (choose from transparent, translucent and opaque)
8. The force that acts on objects thrown upwards
9. The force experienced by like poles of magnets when they are brought closer to each other
10. The energy possessed by an object due to its motion

**B. In each of the following questions, two choices are correct. Identify the correct choices.** **(9 × 2 = 18)**

1. Which of the following causes air pollution?
   (a) Heavy rainfall
   (b) Smoke from the industries
   (c) Washing clothes in a pond
   (d) Oil spill
   (e) Using firewood for cooking
   (f) Loudspeakers
2. Which of the following are igneous rocks?
   (a) Granite
   (b) Shale
   (c) Conglomerate
   (d) Marble
   (e) Pumice
   (f) Slate
3. Which of the following cause flood?
   (a) Heavy rainfall
   (b) Excess usage of groundwater
   (c) Overflowing water bodies
   (d) Creation of larger number of tributaries for rivers
   (e) Less evaporation of sea water
   (f) Large amount of building constructions

4. What are the applications of air pressure in our daily life?
   (a) Windmill (b) Drinking through a straw
   (c) Coffee makers (d) Thermometer
   (e) Vacuum cleaner (f) Water treatment
5. Which of these are translucent materials?
   (a) Spectacles (b) Butter paper (c) Cardboard sheet
   (d) Aquarium bowl (e) Frosted glass (f) Wooden block
6. Which of the following are examples of wheel and axle?
   (a) Doorknob (b) Pulley (c) Axe
   (d) Knife (e) Scissors (f) Bottle opener
7. Force can change the shape of an object. Which of the following are examples of this?
   (a) Blowing air into a balloon
   (b) Goalkeeper stopping a ball in a football match
   (c) Man riding a cycle fast
   (d) Batsman hitting a ball in a cricket match
   (e) Making a model using clay
   (f) Applying brakes in a moving car
8. Rohan and Suman want to measure the length and breadth of one of the floor tiles in their respective houses for comparison. Which of the following units are suitable for measuring them?
   (a) Handspan (b) Metre scale (c) Cubit
   (d) Measuring tape (e) Foot (f) Thumb
9. Which of the following are the units of time measurement?
   (a) Degree Celsius (b) Milligram (c) Days
   (d) Hours (e) Kelvin (f) Metre

**C. Answer the following questions.** **(2 × 3 = 6)**

1. Draw a well-labelled diagram of the interior parts of the Earth.
2. What are metamorphic rocks? Briefly explain any two types of metamorphic rocks.

**D. Answer the following questions in detail.** **(4 × 4 = 16)**

1. Briefly explain the causes and effects of land and water pollution.
2. Describe the process of distillation with the help of a labelled diagram.
3. What are the characteristics of a shadow?
4. Explain measurement. Name the different quantities of measurement with their standard units and measuring devices.

# The Story of Ozone

What is ozone layer? Where is this? I do not see anything from here.
It is high up in the atmosphere; that is why we cannot see it. It prevents harmful rays of the sun from reaching the Earth.
Then, is it like a blanket?
Yes, but now there is a hole in it!
Is the hole a real thing? Oh my god! Now what do we do?
Really? Who made it?
The humans and the pollution they create.
Yes, my children; it is true. Harmful rays from the sun can now reach the Earth through this hole.

What will happen now, Mamma?
Don't worry, human beings are learning from their mistakes. (I am hoping they are!)
Mamma, look, some school children are passing by. What are they doing? And what are they holding in their hands?
Read, my children! They are creating awareness on reducing pollution and saving the Earth.
Say no to plastics! Carry your own cloth bag.
Do not cuttrees; instead, plant new ones.
Reduce the smoke from vehicles; get your vehicle tested regularly.
Do not burn waste, reuse or recycle them.
Do not burn crackers; instead, light a lamp.
Keep your environment clean. Do not litter.
Do not pollute water sources.
Do not waste water. Harvest rainwater.

# Skills You Need

## MARKETING

Have you ever gone shopping for storybooks, shoes, clothes or toys? What do you do first? Firstly, you think about the items that you need. Then, you look for a place or a store where these items would be sold. Next, you think about whether you have the money to buy these items or not. When you reach the store, you look around at the options available. You look at the packaging, colours, features, etc. Finally, you buy what you like the best, if the price is reasonable and you have the money to buy it.

The producers of these items (companies or the people working in such companies where these items are made) think of all these points while developing an item. They think about how best to showcase their items so that buyers like you would buy it. *The activities, such as selling, advertising, packaging, etc., involved in the moving of items from the producer to the buyer is called* ***marketing****.*

### Why Is Marketing Important?

Marketing is everywhere. It is an important tool for the company making the items.

- It helps to attract more people who can buy the items made by the company.
- It is a means for the company to earn more money.
- It provides employment opportunity to many people.

Marketing helps the buyers in many ways.

- It tells people about new items with new features.
- It helps in increasing the standard of living.
- It helps in satisfying human needs and wants.
- It helps ensure stable price of products in the market.

## Career Exploration

- Marketing Manager
- Product Manager
- Advertising or Promotions Manager
- Media Planner
- Public Relations Specialist

## BECOME A MARKETEER

A person who sells items in a market is called a marketer.

**Aim:** Organize a craft fair

**We need:** Papier Mache, colours, glue, scissors, origami sheets, old mugs, bottles, cartons, etc.

**Procedure:**

1. Arrange your class into 4 or 5 groups. Group 1 can make craft items from Papier Mache, old ceramic mugs, cartons, bottles or other items of their choice.
2. Group 2 can find out what type of items are most popular nowadays.
3. Group 3 can calculate the price of the items.
4. Group 4 can think of the various ways of promoting the items. Think of creative ideas with which you can promote the items.
5. The whole class can think of the best suitable space where the items can be displayed for sale such as a classroom, the seminar hall or the school canteen. (*Take permission from your school head/teacher for using any of these spaces. What would you do with the money earned from the sale?*)

## Try it!

Look around your house. Make a list of five items that were bought from the market. Ask your family members a few questions that would help you understand more about marketing. Some sample questions:

- Why did you buy this item?
- What made you buy this item?
- Where did you buy it?
- What was the price of the item?

# Happiness Activity Sheets

## MY GOAL: A HEALTHY LIFE

Most of us think that health is the absence of diseases. Being healthy means not only the absence of disease, but also a state of complete physical, mental and social well-being. Some main factors that contribute to the good health of a person are healthy habits, healthy mental status, healthy relationships and a healthy habitat.

### Healthy Habits

To live a healthy life, one should have a healthy body. To keep our body healthy,

- Eat healthy food.
- Get enough sleep.
- Exercise daily.
- Practice healthy habits such as brushing teeth, bathing, combing hair, clipping nails, etc.
- Maintain personal hygiene.
- Follow a daily routine.

### Healthy Relationships

Healthy relations with our family and friends keep us healthy emotionally too. To have healthy relationships,

- Help and take care of those around you.
- Appreciate your friends.
- Have healthy competition with your classmates.

### Healthy Mental Status

A person full of positivity is said to have a healthy mental status. To achieve sound mental health, think happy and good thoughts.

### Healthy Habitat

Only a healthy habitat can provide us with fresh air, nourishing food and clean drinking water. Human activities have badly affected our environment by polluting air, water and land. So, we should always try to take care of our habitat.

We cannot live a happy life if we are not healthy. A healthy person is more confident and has more courage to achieve success in life. A healthy person enjoys and experiences more pleasure in life. So, it is very important to maintain good health.

**Are you aware of your feelings?**

How do you feel knowing that some of our activities are harming the health of our habitat that eventually affects our health? Write 3–4 words that best describe your feelings in this thought bubble.

**How mindful are you?**

Do you know there are little habits we mindlessly practise every day without even realizing the negative effects these habits have on our health? Reflect and write any such five habits.

How would you rectify these bad habits in order to be healthy?

**What about creating some artwork!**

We all love to give and receive gifts. This small gesture expresses our feeling towards others. This improves our social and emotional well-being and helps to maintain healthy relationships with the people around us.

Use your creativity to design beautiful cards and gift them to your friends expressing how special they are to you. Make a list of friends you would like to give these cards to in the space provided.